SMALL DOJO BIG PROFITS

THE COMPLETE GUIDE TO STARTING AND RUNNING A HIGHLY PROFITABLE MARTIAL ARTS SCHOOL

MIKE MASSIE

MODERN DIGITAL PUBLISHING, AUSTIN, TX

Mike Massie/Modern Digital Publishing
P.O. Box 682
Dripping Springs, TX 78620
www.martialartsbusinessdaily.com

Small Dojo Big Profits/ Michael Massie. —2nd print ed.

ISBN 978-0-9896683-0-9

ABOUT SMALL DOJO BIG PROFITS

For over a decade, Small Dojo Big Profits has guided martial arts instructors through the risky yet highly rewarding process of starting and running a successful and profitable martial art school. Eschewing the conventional wisdom that says you must have a huge school with 300+ students to be financially successful, the author instead shows you how to take on less risk while working smarter not harder by running a lean, mean, efficient martial arts studio operation.

Author Mike Massie has started three successful martial arts studios from scratch, and has the distinction of opening his first studio with no start-up capital, zero credit, and in a town where he was a complete stranger. Yet, he was able to go from teaching in part-time locations to running his own full-time studio in under a year, and did so while staying in profit from month one.

The process he followed is the same one this book is based upon, and this updated version of Small Dojo Big Profits also draws on the author's experience in starting and growing two more successful studios during the recent mortgage crisis and economic recession.

Just think...

...no more time clocks

...no more early morning commute

...and no more working at a job you hate, just so you can support your martial arts training.

Once you learn Mike's step-by-step martial arts business success plan and understand the *right* method to launching a successful martial art school, you may never have to punch a time clock again.

A common sense martial arts school start-up and business operations manual, this completely updated version of the classic martial arts business guide is perfect for anyone who wants to maintain their integrity while building a successful martial art school. If you're looking for the best source of complete information for starting, growing, and running a martial art school from scratch, this is it.

READER PRAISE FOR SMALL DOJO BIG PROFITS:

"I've been teaching Martial Arts as a full time career for over 24 years. I ran a school for my former instructor until very recently and now have a school of my own in Moreno Valley, California. We are doing very well and are way ahead of where we planned to be by this point. The insights you shared in your 'Small Dojo' material helped my transition from instructor/employee to owner/operator. I thank you."

- *Mark O'Dell, Owner, The Training Mat, Moreno Valley, CA*

"My husband and I purchased your book late last year. We are in the process of starting to open a school here in Carlsbad, California. First off, I have to say how much we value your book - it's truly fantastic and worth the price. You have convinced us that a bigger dojang is not the way for us to go. Your advice on billing and consultation is invaluable. Thank you so much."

- *Marguerite Gilvey, Co-owner, AK Karate Carlsbad, CA*

"We are using your book as our Bible! Things are going

good, my two sons are now working with me one full-time and one part-time. We actually have a plan and some short and long term goals. So many thanks!"

- Bob Herten, 8th Dan, Shido-kan Karate, Fair Lawn, NJ

"Small Dojo, Big Profits offers sage advice for people who wish to operate a successful martial arts studio... If you run a dojo or are thinking about starting one, this guide could be the key to your success."

- Regan Carey, Essential Gear Column, Black Belt Magazine

"Excellent! Informative! Enlightening! Small Dojo Big Profits is without a doubt the best book I have ever read on how to run a successful martial arts school. It is nothing but meat & potatoes. This book is designed to help you master the art of 'Fiscal Fitness'."

- Jim McCann, XtremeFreestyle.com

"I have really been loving your book! It has resolved a lot of confusion for us. You break all the basics down into simple language and usable material. You also seem to have completely eliminated the need for huge marketing companies, billing companies, etc. Thanks for putting things into perspective."

- Jason Heriford, Mas Guru, Kali Silat

"I loved your book and told a friend of mine who lives in another province to buy your book. I told him that it was worth every penny spent. He thought the price was somewhat high and I laughed cause I told him I would have paid $300 easily now that I know what this book is actually worth. Thanks!"

- Troy Kaye, Siu Lum Pai, Chinese Boxing Association

"You are completely changing how I market, my confidence as a new school, and as an owner. I purchased your Small Dojo Big Profits text as my first investment when starting out. I can say it is the key to my success."

- Lester Hicks, Chosen Martial Arts Academy

"I'm opening a martial arts school using your book... It is amazing what is falling into place. I'm doing this with virtually nothing, I've barely started, but all the indicators are off the hook. Good job. Your attitude towards this is EXACTLY what I was looking for - a sustainable model vs. a treadmill."

- Joe Judt, Studio Garuda

Dedicated to Deanna and Caleb

"Praise be to the Lord my Rock,
who trains my hands for war,
my fingers for battle."

PSALM 144:1

PREFACE

THE SMALL DOJO BIG PROFITS MINDSET AND METHOD

Within these pages, you'll find the distillation of the business knowledge I have gained through nearly thirty years of martial arts training, twenty-five-plus years of teaching the martial arts, and twenty years of teaching in my own studios as a professional martial arts instructor. Along with that experience, I have spent countless hours attending college business courses and industry seminars, as well as studying manuals and texts pertaining both to the business aspects of martial arts instruction and business topics in general. While I did all this, I was also attending the school of hard knocks, where I had a seat in the front row.

As you might imagine, the information I share in this manual did not come cheap; it was hard-won, well-earned, and it is simply impossible to put a real price on what it cost me to get it. Fortunately for you, you won't have to go through what I went through to learn how to run a successful studio because you can learn from my mistakes and triumphs and bypass much of the trials and tribulations I went through, simply by following the advice and instructions in this manual.

Undoubtedly, some of you who read this book will already be

familiar with many of the techniques and business methods described herein; others of you who are newer to the industry will likely learn something new on every page. Yet, in my humble opinion, whether you are a veteran studio owner or a brand new instructor, you will find something of value within these pages. Even the smallest idea or twist on an approach can breathe new life into your existing operations, and even slight adjustments and improvements in each area of a business can add up over time to serious increases in the bottom line.

Still, I believe that the biggest value to be found in this book is not so much in the business techniques I describe for you to use in your own studio, but in the fact that most every approach I mention has been used to a degree of success in my own operations. Unlike some of the advice you will get from certain "experts" in our indus-try, you will not be the subject of someone's martial arts business experiment when you follow the instructions in this book. Instead, you will be using methods that I have found to be tried and true, and that have proven to work well in other industries besides our own.

In addition, I know that some will read this book and be put off by my scathing remarks as to the state of the martial arts industry in America. As far as that goes, I will tell you outright that I critique everyone with equal impunity; at the very least I am fair in that regard. Please do not assume that I am merely spouting negative and facetious diatribe for its own sake. I sincerely believe that there exists a real and serious problem with the powers that be in the martial arts industry today, and I am more than willing to bring attention to what I believe are problems of major proportions that, if left unchecked, will ruin our industry.

Since I have experienced the negative repercussions of the very issues I confront in this text in running my own studios, I feel that I am categorically qualified to make these assertions. In order that you should avoid making the same mistakes I have made, my advice to you would be to question everything you hear and read regarding martial arts business practices. Because, as the ancient scholars said, "ubi dubium ibi libertas" or "Where there is doubt, there is freedom."

This Method Works

One thing I would like to say about the methods I promote in this book is that they work. I wouldn't lie to you or mislead you; I have no reason to do so. Once again, this book is a collection of the best ideas and methods that I have come across and used in my twenty years of professionally teaching the martial arts. Use them, and you will meet with success, I can assure you of it.

When I tell you that owning a small studio is better than running a large mega-studio, you can take it to heart that I know this from personal experience. But, I don't want you to think that my way is the only way to be successful; it isn't. With regards to other methods and approaches to school management that encourage you to open a large studio, to enroll as many students as you can cram into it, and hire a large staff to run things, I am not going to lie to you and tell you that there aren't people in this industry that are making money that way. In fact, I will tell you that there are people in this industry who are making a great deal of money using those methods. But, those people are few and far between.

My experience, education, and observations have taught me that having a large studio makes it much more difficult for an *inexperienced* studio owner to succeed. I know that may sound backwards to you, because many of you who are reading this have been conditioned to equate large school size with financial success, so let me explain. You have to do a lot more work in a large studio, and you have a lot more headaches. Running a large studio requires much more operating capital and manpower to run, which will cut into your profit margin. Large studios require that you hire and train many employees, and that brings a whole list of issues into the mix that you don't need at this juncture.

I admit, if you are an exceptional leader, with above average management, marketing, and organizational skills, then you will most likely do extremely well and be highly successful running a large studio. But, if you are like most of the martial artists I know and currently only possess average skill and experience in these areas, you are much better off starting small and learning how to get the most out of a modest studio operation, instead of trying to become a martial arts tycoon before you have gained the experience or know-how to run a smaller business successfully.

Pareto's Principle

There is a principle in business called the Pareto principle, which was first discovered by an Italian economist named Vilfredo Pareto. Pareto's principle states that 80% of your results will be derived from 20% of your efforts. My advice to those who are just starting out is that you stick to the methods I present in this book until you can do them in your sleep, because 80% of your business success will come from knowing and applying the simple principles of martial arts business management that I outline in this book.

I would also like to add that if you apply Pareto's principle with regards to the issue of school size and enrollment you will find that you can easily achieve 80% of the financial success of a large martial arts studio with only 20% of the resources they expend. Think on that concept as you read through this manual; it will save you a good deal of stress, frustration, and disappointment if you learn to apply that simple concept in your martial arts business.

Mike Massie
Austin, Texas
July, 2013

INTRODUCTION

OR, WHY I WROTE THIS BOOK

This book was specifically written to be a step-by-step guide for opening a *highly profitable* martial arts studio. And although it was written with the newcomer in mind, there is much of value for the seasoned studio owner within these pages as well. I labored long and hard in writing this book, and make a sincere effort throughout to provide a complete system for opening and operating a successful and profitable martial arts school. Whether you are just starting out or you have been in business for some time, you will find something of interest and value within these pages.

Unfortunately, many of us that got started in this business over the last few decades never had a manual such as this one to guide us on our journey. And, although there is now a plethora of information on the subject of running a martial arts studio, much of it leaves something to be desired with regards to the application of ethics and sound business principles. For your benefit, I will explain the reasons for this, as I see them, in great detail over the next few pages. Hold on to your hats, folks, because this is going to be a bumpy ride.

Like Sheep to the Slaughter

Contrary to what you might think, there really aren't that many martial arts studio owners turning a decent profit these days. As a person who has been directly involved in running a studio for the last two decades, and as one who has been coaching martial arts school owners for more than half of that time, I can tell you for a fact there are a lot of school owners who are struggling to make ends meet, despite what you may have read in the magazines or heard at the conventions. Quite frankly, it is my strongly held opinion that this can be directly attributed to the abundance of bad business information (or *misinformation*, depending on how you look at it) floating around today in our industry.

If you disagree with me, I invite you to go to any martial arts industry seminar or workshop and listen; I mean *really* listen, to the presenters. By reading between the lines and comparing what they say, you will find that much of the time they contradict each other, give their audience information that is untested and untried (*"Sure I'll come speak at your event, I need some fresh guinea pigs that will be willing to try my new untested marketing idea out for me!"*), and generally give advice that works to their benefit, not yours (*"Of course you need to teach Combat Para-Military Hand-to-Hand Killing Techniques of the Latvian Special Forces in your studio! Did you sign up for my certification class later? It's only $249 per person, this weekend only!"*).

Sadly, few of the big names in our industry are looking out for the little guy, the one who doesn't want to own a 500, 750, or 1,200 student martial arts super center with a staff of twenty and yearly overhead expenses that could put the entire nation of Lichtenstein through Harvard. The reason for this is simple: the big businesses that service martial arts schools realized a long time ago that the bigger operations generate more profit as customers.

Let me qualify that statement. Specifically, the billing companies make more money if a studio has more students to bill; the equipment suppliers make more money if there are more students to buy their wares; and the consulting companies and "industry associations" make more money if schools have more staff members to attend their business training seminars. So, the big players in the industry are more than happy to propagate the belief that "bigger schools are better." But as you will observe, it is my strongly held opinion that embracing this idea is perhaps the worst mistake a studio owner can make.

This idea that bigger schools are better was virtually crammed down my throat during my first decade as a professional martial arts instructor and school owner. Yet, I always had nagging suspicions that something about the idea just didn't add up. Every time someone tried to convince me that running a larger studio was the best way to go, I always came back to the same two questions:

1. *"What are the benefits of having a school of over 300 students?"*
2. *"Is it possible to teach a quality martial arts program on that large of a scale?"*

In answer to the first question, I have found that the answer generally relates to holding bragging rights among your fellow school owners, which has little if anything to do with having a better quality of life. But is that really the measure of our success, bragging rights to who has the most students? Ask around among people who are running operations of 500-plus students and you'll soon find that they aren't making that much more *net profit* than the guy or gal who runs an efficient 250 student school – *yet they are working twice as hard!* This stands as a clear and shining testament to the validity of the economic principle known as the Law of Diminishing Returns.

When the economy goes south (and it will again, eventually, as we know from observing economic trends) and students start dropping out by the droves, who do you think will survive? Will it be the guy with the 8,500 square foot studio that has monthly overhead costs to match the gross national product of a small Third-World country, or the little guy in the postage-stamp school who makes a tidy profit every month by keeping his overhead and expenses to a bare minimum? I think you know the answer.

As far as the second question regarding school size is concerned, my experience and observations have led me to the conclusion that the answer is generally "no", with some rare exceptions. You simply cannot maintain world-class quality on a large scale. Just look at the fast-food industry and you will see a prime example of this axiom. Sure, they have efficient methods of making and serving their food, but the best thing you can say for their quality is that they are, without exception, consistently mediocre. Now, think about how this relates to the quality of martial arts that you desire to pass on to your students. Do you really want to be forever known as the instructor who founded "McDojo International?"

On a related topic, I strongly hold to the belief that not everyone is cut out to be a black belt. But, achieving black belt is the "carrot" that the industry suggests we dangle in front of our students to keep them coming to class. As you might have guessed, many school owners have found this to be a double-edged sword. To keep retention high, you have to entice your students with the reward of achieving ever-increasing rank. Yet, in order to retain a clientele made up of larger and larger segments of the population you must in some way compromise the necessary performance standards required to earn that rank.

Allow me to explain exactly what I mean. For example, you can't expect the average eight-year-old to be able to learn long and complicated forms or to understand and verbalize the deeper philosophies that underlie the arts. You shouldn't expect a 90-pound co-ed to be able to fight full-contact for three hard rounds with 200-pound men in the sparring ring. And you certainly can't expect a 55-year-old sedentary office jockey to be able to perform jump-spinning hook kicks and a center split.

I realize that these examples may not be indicative of your style or system. But, I am fairly certain that there *are* aspects of the martial arts style you practice and teach that are considered to be standard fare for black belts in your system, that some segments of the general population could not be reasonably be expected to learn or perform. Sadly, by lowering those standards so that the "average" person can achieve black belt, we as an industry have lowered the bar so far that the rank no longer holds any real significance in the modern commercial dojo.

Now, the good news is that you don't have to fall into this trap. In fact, you can run a successful and profitable martial arts studio without handing out black belts like sparklers at a 4th of July picnic. I myself ran my first studio for a decade and only promoted a handful of students to black belt during that time. Furthermore, I would point to the growing popularity of Brazilian jiu-jitsu, where a student will typically remain a white belt for one or two years before being promoted to blue belt.

The public isn't stupid. Certainly, there will always be a market for people who want the easy route to black belt. However, there are just as many people who want to learn quality martial arts and who also desire the challenge of earning something by 'paying the iron price," as one prominent traditional martial artist recently described it. So, don't be misled into believing that you have to sell out to be successful as a school owner. Nothing could be further from the truth.

The More Things Change, the More They Stay the Same

A decade or so ago when I first wrote this book, combination billing and consulting companies were all the rage. It seemed that every large martial arts school used one, and their owners were more than happy to tell everyone to become a client. Typically, these folks were on the "board of directors" or some such, which explains at least in part why they were so eager to tell other school owners to give away 7-10% of their gross income a month to a billing company for something they could easily handle in-house. At any rate, back then my major grief was with these companies, since being in the "we collect your student tuition" business and the "we tell you how to run your school" business at the same time is a major conflict of interest. In my opinion, this resulted in a lot of school owners receiving a lot of bad advice that hurt their businesses.

Fast forward to today; now, martial arts billing companies have taken a back seat to multiple "industry associations" that are backed by equipment vendors, curriculum licensors, and martial art school franchises. Well, I don't have to tell you that there's a similar conflict of interest when the people telling you how to run your business are also in the business of say, selling martial arts school franchises or selling martial arts equipment. Now, I'm not saying that the information these associations and organizations are handing out is all bad; all I'm saying is that you need to consider the source. It doesn't take a rocket scientist to figure out that they have an agenda that goes beyond helping you succeed as a school owner. So, I suggest you let *caveat emptor* be the rule of the day when dealing with these companies and organizations.

The Small Dojo Big Profits Mindset

The Small Dojo Big Profits Mindset: *A martial art business approach that values deriving maximum financial benefits from minimal financial expenditures and labor outputs above all other metrics and outcomes.*

If you wish to survive in today's economy, you simply cannot afford to follow the herd and rely on some industry "expert" to tell you what is best for you and your business. You must instead be smart, whip smart, and willing to go in the direction that your heart and good sense tell you to go for your own well-being. In addition, you have to apply common sense and use good business practices when dealing with the decisions that will make or break you in business.

Or, stated simply, you have to get into what I call the "Small Dojo Big Profits" mindset. The "Small Dojo Big Profits" mindset is not about having the largest, fanciest, most extravagant studio; it's not about having the most students; it's not even about making the most money. Instead, it is about deriving maximum financial benefits from minimal financial expenditures and labor outputs. It is all about keeping your costs and workload down to a bare minimum while maximizing your gross income in order to ensure that you are reaping the very highest levels of net profit and other benefits from your business.

Important Point: *The simplest way to become successful in this industry is to start a small, highly profitable studio that you can run on your own. Remember, keep it small, and keep it all.*

In order to teach you this mindset, I have gone to great lengths to make this manual as complete as possible. I have done my absolute best to share what I learned in my ten years of running a studio and teaching professionally; the same approach that allowed me to earn a comfortable living while averaging an active student count of only 150 students and working just 25 hours a week on average in my studio. In this book, I will teach you this approach so you can make a very comfortable living just like I have, without all the long hours, hassles, and headaches that go with having a huge 300+ student studio. In addition, you will learn the truth about being successful in the martial arts industry, and you may even redefine your own idea of what success means along the way.

However, accomplishing this task will require that you commit to having both a positive attitude and an open mind while you read through this manual. You are going to have to "empty your cup" and forget much of what you have been told about what defines a successful martial arts studio. In doing so, you can rest assured that I do care about your success, and will only advise you to do something if it has worked for me. Rather than give you a bunch of ideas I read in a book somewhere, I am going to tell you exactly what myself and others have done and are still doing to achieve great success in running our martial arts studios while avoiding unnecessary work and risk.

But just reading about these strategies is not enough; you have to be willing to get out and implement them to your benefit. As others have said before, it is not the acquisition of knowledge that gives you an advantage in your endeavors, but instead it is the dutiful application of the knowledge you have gained that will ensure your success. Therefore, I recommend that you study these ideas and concepts carefully; until they are imprinted in your memory, so that implementing them will become a reflexive habit for you.

And If You're Just Starting Out...

In addition to reading this book, I want you to do some additional research before you start your studio. Go out and interview school owners that you know, introduce yourself to the ones you don't know, network with their associates, ask them how they do things, what works for them, what their budget and profit-margins are like, and so on.

Read books on the topic, then read, read, and read some more. Listen to audios on general business and success topics. Take some classes and seminars in business and management at your local college. Go ahead and attend the industry seminars, while filtering what you hear through your best B.S. detector.

All of these efforts will add up to ensure that when you do open your school, you won't risk your success by falling for some fad or trend, or by listening to bad advice from the wrong people. In short, I want you to *learn to think for yourself*.

Quite honestly, if you work hard enough and apply what you learn, it almost doesn't matter whose advice you follow - you *will* be successful. However, if you listen to me, you'll be successful *and* have time to enjoy a life outside of your martial arts studio.

Who This Book Is NOT Written For...

Let me take a moment to tell you who this book *IS NOT* written for. This book is not for the close-minded, the brainwashed, the gullible, nor is it for those without a sense of humor or who take themselves too seriously. This book is not written for the industry puppets that are compensated handsomely to endorse less-than-ethical companies and substandard products. Nor is it for those who promote their students to black belt in a pre-determined period of time regardless of their knowledge, skill level, or performance.

It is not written for the 25-year-old who promoted himself or herself to 10th dan, or who touts themselves as a self-appointed *soke*, *shihan*, *hanshi*, *dojunim*, grandmaster, or any of the myriad ridiculous titles being used these days ("supreme great grandmaster" comes to mind), nor is it written for the many who become founders of new martial arts "systems" after only five or ten years of training a few hours a week. It is not written for anyone who flat out *WORSHIPS* their instructor (or anyone else for that matter), nor for any of those spineless souls who obey the senior people in their style or system with unflinching and unquestioning compliance, regardless of the impact their decisions and actions have on others.

Nor is it written for those power-hungry "masters" who use suggestions and inferences of their supposed mystical *chi* powers, their high rank, or their position of influence to manipulate the minds of their students for their own ego's sake (or in order that they may lead them down the path of lightening their wallets instead of enlightening their minds).

In short, if any of the above applies to you, then this book is not for you. Put it down right now and walk away before reading it gives you a stroke (on second thought, keep reading – maybe you will have a stroke and we'll be left with one less knucklehead in our industry).

Who This Book Is Written For

Now, let me tell you who this book IS written for. It is written for the instructor who has been struggling to make ends meet, working a full-time job while trying to keep their studio open. It is written for the person who teaches at the local recreation center because they love working with kids, or battered women, or the elderly, or just plain teaching people period, and who has serious dreams of owning a studio someday.

It is written for the person who has suffered ridicule from their family and friends because of their decision to teach the martial arts as a full-time profession. It is for anyone who has ever been told, "You can't make any money doing that!" as well as for those who are simply tired of being told "you can't" by their friends, family, and co-workers.

This book is also written for those school owners who keep beating their heads against the wall, wondering why they can't get their enrollment up to 500 students in a single location like the "superstars" who are on the covers of the latest industry magazines. Or, in an even worse scenario, it is written for those who are making less net profit and much lower profit margins than they were previously because they actually *did* reach the 500 student mark, or because they took some bad advice and opened multiple locations. And, let's not forget those who suddenly find that they have no life outside of their studio because they are spending all their time managing a huge enrollment and/or multiple locations.

It is also written for school owners who are tired of the exorbitant fees that martial arts billing companies charge, which are generally five to ten times higher than the standard in other similar industries. It is written for those who have been flat-out lied to and misled by certain martial arts business consultants, and it is for those of us who just can't bring ourselves to implement the sales tactics and marketing tools that those people have suggested we use, because we find them to be unethical and just plain distasteful.

And finally, it is written for those who have crossed over to the "dark-side" by doing everything their billing company or consultant told them to do, implementing bait-and-switch, high-pressure and hard-sell tactics in their studios, but yet who have at least retained a small shred of decency (or common sense) and want to come back over to the good side of the "force." I have "been there, done that" and I know what you are going through.

If any of this applies to you and your situation, I hope you enjoy this book.

Acknowledgements

I'd like to thank all the school owners and instructors who told others about this book; I sincerely appreciate your support during the last decade. I'd also like to acknowledge all the instructors I've trained with over the years, who are too numerous to name. Finally, I'd like to thank those people who were caring enough to share their business knowledge and wisdom with me. Again, you are too numerous to name, but I thank you for your generosity.

ONE

"ARE YOU CRAZY? YOU CAN'T MAKE ANY MONEY DOING THAT!"

"Keep away from people who try to belittle your ambitions. Small people always do that, but the really great make you feel like you, too, can become great."

MARK TWAIN

Save Us from Those Who Would Save Us...

"Are you nuts? You can't make a living teaching martial arts!" Boy, if I had a dollar for every time someone told me that, I'd have the down payment on a new Mercedes. I remember when I first decided I wanted to teach the martial arts as a profession. I was a typical teenage martial arts junkie, at the *dojo* four nights a week between my own training and assisting my *sensei* (really, I would have been there more often, but it was only open four nights week). I wanted to be a black belt so bad I could taste it, and my dream was to someday open my own studio and teach karate for a living.

Before I was able to test for *shodan*, however, my family circumstances changed and I moved to another state for a while to live with my relatives. Finding a place to train was no problem, but I would have to switch styles back to *tae kwon do* from *Shotokan* and train at my old instructor's school, which really didn't bother me; he was a talented instructor and I respected him a great deal, so I was more than happy to continue my studies with him. Unfortunately, that's when the "dream-stealers" showed up.

The "Mushroom Mindset"

Amazingly, it started with my instructor of the time. Unfortunately, he was constantly putting other instructors down in order to boost his own ego and to improve his standing with his students, which in hindsight was a really tragic thing to witness. Never mind that the guy was so darn *good* at what he did that his students would have thought that he walked on water no matter what he said. Some folks just don't know what they have, you know?

Now, I don't have a problem with calling a duck a duck; if it walks like a phony and quacks like a phony then it's a phony. However, this instructor just had to knock all of the other instructors around town and everything that they did. If they competed in certain tournaments, he criticized them; if they did flashy demos, he criticized them; if they wore colored uniforms instead of plain white ones, he criticized them - he basically criticized everything except for what he did in his own school. And, surprise, surprise; he was especially sensitive to the actions of the guy who had the most successful school in town. In fact, he probably spent more time criticizing this guy than he did anyone else.

Before you start thinking that he was a total jerk, let me give you a little background on him and his relationship with the people he trained under, because they were some real characters and probably the source of his bad attitude toward other instructors. For one thing, no matter how well you knew these guys, they had a strict policy of "no testing fee, no promotion." I mean, these guys were stingy with rank; a person might wait years and years to be promoted under them, unless they had enough money to test. Not that I think anyone should give rank away for free, but there are other ways of paying for a rank promotion, such as by displaying loyalty and commitment to your instructors, which my instructor had shown abundantly.

Yet, instead of promoting him to a higher rank as a reward for his hard-earned skill and knowledge, they instead convinced him that he was incapable of testing and promoting his own students, presumably so they could be assured of keeping all the money there was to be made on ranking those students. My best guess is that because of the indoctrination he received from his instructors, in his mind, it was okay to make money teaching the martial arts, but you just couldn't make *too much* money unless you were a "real master instructor" (whatever *that* means). Since this other guy in town didn't fit his idea of what a "real" martial arts master was, in his eyes he was a fake and didn't deserve the money he was making at his studio.

As you might guess, he passed his co-dependent mindset on to his students. And that's how I became indoctrinated into believing one of the biggest philosophical lies that has ever disgraced the martial arts world. Of course, I am speaking of the stupid and totally unfounded idea that, unless you are a super-high-ranking master instructor (or Asian, which of course *automatically* qualifies you as an expert, *wink-wink*), a martial arts instructor should never, ever, ever become wealthy from teaching the martial arts. I mean, heaven forbid that a second or third degree black belt would actually get paid well for sharing their hard-earned knowledge and experience with others. Instead, according to this philosophy, lower-ranking martial arts instructors are supposed to kow-tow to their "masters" and teach for free (and preferably at their instructors' studios). What a load of bull!

As ridiculous as this may sound to some of you, to this day I continue to meet experienced martial arts instructors who not only accept this type of treatment from the people they train under, they also inflict the same backwards thinking on their own black belts. Or, to use an old cliché, they "treat them like mushrooms, feeding them crap and keeping them in the dark." Certainly, this begs the question, "Whatever happened to empowering people through the martial arts?" Yet, I digress; let's get back to my early adventures in overcoming the "dream stealers."

Important Point: *Your rank has nothing to do with your income potential.*

So I Decided to Open My Own Studio...

It would be years after that experience before I got that stupid idea out of my system. Even more dream-stealers showed up a few years later when I was in college. Incidentally, I ended up attending college just to get my parents out of my hair, which was why I joined the military as well. At the time, neither the military nor the college environment offered what I really wanted – a career teaching the martial arts. However, I chose the path of least resistance, rather than hear my family complain about how I was "wasting my time" on all that kung-fu malarkey. After getting out of the military in '92, I let my friends and family convince me that I should go to nursing school, because nurses were in high demand. To this day, I have tremendous respect for nurses, don't get me wrong, but I was miserable in nursing school. I dropped out in the first semester, despite earning straight "A's" in all my classes.

When I made the announcement that I was going to open a martial arts school, I got nothing but blank stares and a bunch of "are you stupid?' looks from my loved ones. Never one to be deterred, I promptly went out and found a vacant storefront location in nearby town where no one was teaching the martial arts, dumped several hundred dollars into paint and building supplies to fix it up, spent three weeks or so working on the place, and then allowed my friends and family to discourage me out of actually opening the doors to the public. The score was now Dream-stealers, 2; me, 0.

To everyone's amazement but my own, the urge to become a full-time martial arts instructor never left me. In fact, I only managed to hold it back for about a year or so. Finally, in February of 1994, I quit my near-minimum wage job in the healthcare industry and left my girlfriend and everything I knew behind to pursue a career teaching the martial arts in Austin, Texas. My family and friends pretty much freaked out, and my girlfriend at that time was quoted to me as saying, *"What is he thinking? You can't make any money doing that!"* Despite the many protests at home, with only $50 in my pocket, an old broken-down car, what few belongings I had that fit in the car, and the name and address of my instructor's instructor, I took the leap for good.

The original plan was that I would help my instructor's former instructor to launch a new school in North Austin. That plan didn't last very long. Let's just say that I had some real philosophical differences with that guy as to the ethical standards martial arts instructors should uphold (like I said, these guys were some real characters). Not wanting to be involved in someone else's scandals, I got a job working nights at a gas station and soon moved on.

After a few weeks, I worked out a deal with the community education office in a nearby town and started teaching in the elementary school gym two nights a week. Finally, I was getting paid to teach my own students, and I was on cloud nine. For the first time in my life, I had beaten the dream-stealers.

But, that was just the beginning; little did I know that there was a lot more to becoming a successful professional martial arts instructor than just securing a location and showing up to teach. It would be two more years until I had the financial resources, business acumen, and know-how to open a full-time location. In fact, what I learned in those two years makes up the bulk of what I will cover in this book.

The great thing for you is that it won't take you two years, or even two months to learn what you need to know to open your own studio.

I am going to lay it all out for you, so that by the time you finish reading this book you will know exactly what you need to do to become successful in the martial arts industry, *without* compromising your morals and ethics and while still having a life outside of your studio. You get to experience all the benefits of being able to implement the lessons I learned during that difficult time period, without having to slug through the mud and muck like I did to learn them.

Important Point: *Learn from the mistakes of others to accelerate your own journey to personal success.*

TWO
DISPELLING THE MYTHS THAT SURROUND OUR INDUSTRY

In This Industry, Myths Abound...

Before we get into the nuts and bolts of starting a martial arts school, I want to make sure that you have a clear understanding of the TRUTH about being successful as a professional martial arts instructor. Like I said in the introduction, there is definitely a lot of B.S. being spread around as the gospel truth in the martial arts industry, for whatever reason. I want to clear things up for you right here and now, so you can get started on the right foot today, and not be sent on some wild goose chase when you start your business.

Myth #1

"All REAL martial arts instructors (or traditionalists, or purists) teach for free, or they don't make their primary income teaching the martial arts, or they don't have a commercial studio, etc."

As I wrote in the last chapter, this idea and others similar to it are pure cow manure. Historically, martial artists have always been paid, and paid very well, to teach their art to others. In pre-20th century Japan, samurai were often employed and paid handsomely to teach their craft. In a more modern example, consider the fact that Bruce Lee was known to have charged $275 per hour tuition for private instruction. In today's dollars, that's about $1,800 an hour!

Let me offer you a common analogy to more effectively illustrate my position. I think most experienced martial artists would agree that a martial arts instructor who has earned a legitimate teaching credential and rank should have roughly six to ten years of their life invested in serious martial arts study and practice learning their craft. I think that everyone will also agree that a similar investment of time and effort in another professional pursuit would have earned that instructor an advanced university degree (think four years for an undergraduate degree, and another two to six years to earn a masters or PhD).

Because of this, I strongly believe that a good martial arts instructor should make an income similar to that of a highly paid professional such as a doctor or lawyer. By the way, in case you are already running a martial arts studio and you are not making that much money, don't worry! I actually wrote this book as a manual for both new instructors and seasoned school owners. I will give you a sound plan that will allow you to achieve your financial dreams through your current business, without selling out.

As for what you should charge to make this amount, we'll get to that in Chapter 8: "Pricing Your Services and Enrolling Students."

Important Point: *You deserve to make the same amount of money as any highly trained professional.*

Myth #2

"All I have to do is open my doors, and all the world will come running to take my classes because I am a: world champion; black belt; high-ranking black belt; head of a martial arts system; well-known expert; etc."

I don't want to burst your balloon, but if you think this is true you are sadly mistaken. The fact is that most people don't give a whit about your accomplishments as a martial artist. To fill your studio, you will need a super marketing plan and phenomenal public relations to boost your image as a community leader. That's what I am going to teach you in Chapter 10: "Marketing on a Budget."

Important Point: *You must learn and implement effective marketing strategies and techniques if you are to succeed in your business.*

Myth #3

"I need a billing company to be successful because so-and-so uses such-and-such billing company and he credits them with his success."

Once again, cow manure and horse hockey. I know of several successful dojo owners that don't spend a penny on outsourcing martial arts billing collection services and they do just fine. One of them, a large studio owner I know in St. Louis, has a student body of well over 500 and handles his own billing quite satisfactorily.

Although I once recommended that studio owners hire a discount billing company to handle their student billing, these days I suggest that you instead set up your own billing system using the latest technology and software. This is a much more cost-effective and sensible option, and it will save you both money and headaches. I am going to tell you exactly how to do this in Chapter 9: "How to Get Your Money without Giving It Away."

As for consulting services, I do recommend that you use a consulting firm, just so long as you make sure that it has no financial connection whatsoever to the company that handles your tuition collections. There is an obvious conflict of interest when your billing company is telling you how to run your business. Don't fall into this trap. I'll tell you exactly which consulting companies I think offer the best service for the small dojo owner in Chapter 3: "Listen to the Right People."

Important Point: *You don't want to use a billing company that charges too much or that offers "free" business advice as part of their billing services.*

Myth #4
   "It takes a lot of up-front cash to start a martial arts studio. I need to take out a loan from my (bank, credit union, private investors, family and friends) to get started."

No way! You can get started from scratch with very little money, if you know what you are doing. Actually, I believe that this is the BEST way to get started in business. Best-selling financial author and millionaire Robert G. Allen agrees with me; in fact, he says that the worst mistake most new business owners make is to be over-capitalized, because when you have gobs of money to start a business, you end up being very inefficient in your spending habits and budgeting. Starting from scratch allows you the "pleasure" of learning how to create and hold on to streams of income.

I'll show you how to do this in Chapter 4: "Financing, The Old Fashioned Way" and in Chapter 5: "Avoiding Legal Pitfalls."

Important Point: *You don't need a lot of money to start a martial arts school, if you are willing to work.*

Myth #5

"I have to have at least (300, 400, 500, 1000) students to make a decent income and really be successful as a martial arts school owner."

Okay, here's one of my pet peeves. You go to a martial arts event, be it a tournament, seminar, business convention, or whatever, and you see a fellow studio owner. When talk comes around to business (which it always does), the first words from this person's mouth are "What's your active count?"

Trust me, I've read the manuals, seen the videos, attended the seminars, spoken with the experts, and heard the sound of one hand clapping (okay, that last one I just put in there for grins). After all that, and in all my years of experience running a martial arts studio, I have never seen any evidence that having a huge studio with 300 or more students makes you a better, more talented, more successful, or happier instructor. In fact, from what I have seen and experienced, I have to say that it is much better to have a studio with 150 students and a profit margin of 70% than a studio with 300 students and a profit margin of 30%. And, the numbers agree with me.

Think I'm full of it? I'm not the only martial arts business veteran who has figured this out. Disregard my advice and you'll soon see that running a super-large studio operation may not be the wisest business plan in today's economy. Later on in this book, I will explain in great detail how having a large enrollment means having more overhead expenses due to the need for a larger studio (higher rent), a larger staff (higher payroll expenses), increased insurance costs, and so forth, and all of these added expenses cut into your net profit and decrease your profit margins.

Another thing to consider is the increased time and energy it takes to manage a large student body of over 250 students. Time and again, I have seen studio owners put on a cheery smile to speak at conventions about how they are so happy that their studios have grown 300% due to the advice they got from ABC Billing Company, but behind the scenes they are working 80 hour weeks and their personal life is in a shambles because of the long hours they spend in their studio. If you want to have a large studio, fine, but you had better plan on sacrificing your free time and your social and family life to keep it going.

I'll cover this and related issues in Chapter 6: "Location, Location, Location = $$$, $$$, $$$", Chapter 7: "Business Plans & Budgeting, a.k.a. Being a Cheap Son-of-a-Gun", and in Chapter 11: "Now That You Have Them, How Are You Going to Keep them?"

Important Point: Smaller is better. Really, it is.

Myth #6
   "I have to have a big staff to help me run my studio."

This is wrong on so many levels I just don't know where to begin. I guess I can start by pointing out the fact that you only need two people to operate a small dojo during normal business hours; an instructor and an office employee. No matter what someone tells you to the contrary, you can indeed get by with a staff of only two or three people (including yourself) when you run a small studio. I will show you the systems I used to do this successfully in Chapter 13: "The Why's and How's of Hiring and Training Help."

I will say that it is nice to have someone to handle things so you can take it easy once in a while. However, payroll and other employee costs can end up being your biggest expense when running a small business (I'll cover this in Chapter 7: "Business Plans & Budgeting, a.k.a. Being a Cheap Son-of-a-Gun").

Also, employees are a major pain in the rear! They call in sick, waste time goofing off (your time, work hours that you are paying them for), they complain and argue amongst themselves, they get injured on the job (which will cost you money, even if they have insurance) and they take nearly as much time to train and manage as they free up for you. In my opinion and experience, having a large staff is more trouble than it's worth.

Important Point: *You don't need a huge staff to run your small studio.*

Myth #7
   "My school must be a storefront location in an expensive, high-foot-traffic shopping center to be successful."

Once again, this is more malarkey. I have spoken with many highly successful studio owners who built 250+ student enrollments in the worst possible locations you can imagine. Some examples include a basement (hard to get to), an upstairs location over a gas station (weird place to put a school *and* hard to get to), a school located in the back of a commercial building (no street signage or exposure), and an industrial park outside of town (where *nobody* goes on normal everyday business).

While it is true that each of these locations lacked foot-traffic and exposure, they all had one distinct and very attractive advantage that a storefront shopping plaza location does not: *low rent*. One *BIG* difference that distinguishes my business system from all the rest is that it is based on being lean and mean, not fat and wasteful. Saving money on your rent means that you can use that money for other more efficient and productive purposes. I'll show you how to find little location gems like these in Chapter 6: "Location, Location, Location = $$$, $$$, $$$."

My own small yet very profitable studio was located in the *middle* of an old run-down plaza, with very little foot traffic. Visitors had to walk down a long confusing access hallway to even get to my place, which had no windows or external exposure (I affectionately called it "The Bat Cave"). My neighbors included two government agriculture offices, a hair salon that catered to old ladies from the local retirement community, an antique (read: junk) shop, and a pharmacy.

Not exactly the best location I could have picked as far as foot-traffic and exposure goes. In fact, most people who drove by couldn't see my sign because the tree foliage along the street blocked the view! Yet, through using effective marketing and public relations techniques I was able to consistently fill my classes year after year. I'll show you how I did it in Chapter 10: "Marketing on a Budget."

Important Point: You don't need to have a large studio in an expensive lease space to be successful.

Myth #8

"I don't need to know anything about standard business and accounting practices to be successful; all I need to know is how to teach good classes."

Yeah, keep thinking that way and we'll be seeing you in the soup kitchen line at the Salvation Army this Christmas. Better than 90% of all small businesses will fail, and most of the time their failure can be attributed to a lack of basic business management skills. Just the fact that you are reading this book shows that you are probably not going to become part of that statistic. However, I could write reams of pages on the various business topics that a business owner must be familiar with, and still not adequately prepare you for every situation you will face.

Want to be a long-term success and not some flash-in-the-pan? You'll need to continually read books and attend seminars on accounting, advertising, marketing, tax laws, business law, and more, for as long as you own your studio. The good news is that I'll tell you where you can go to get all this information and more *absolutely free of charge* in Chapter 3: "Listen to the Right People", and I'll tell you how to avoid potential legal problems in Chapter 5: "Avoiding Legal Pitfalls."

Important Point: *You must learn all you can about business and management to ensure your success.*

Myth #9
    "I don't need a business plan if I'm not borrowing any money. I'll just play it by ear and worry about budgeting later when I am making money."

Fail to plan, plan to fail. Having a business plan and budget is absolutely vital to your success in business. A business plan is like your roadmap for getting to where you want to go. You must set a budget for your business expenditures based on your goals and anticipated income in order to avoid spending too much or too little money on any one area of your business.

What most people don't realize is that there are certain percentages of your gross income that you *MUST* spend on areas such as advertising and marketing every single month to become successful and to keep that momentum rolling once you start getting a steady stream of students. I'll give you an exact plan to follow to ensure your success as you build your business in Chapter 7: "Business Plans & Budgeting, a.k.a. Being a Cheap Son-of-a-Gun."

Important Point: *Fail to plan, and plan to fail.*

Myth #10
  "I'll be able to spend all my time training, once I open my studio."

This is my favorite one, which is why I saved it for last. I have to give a little chuckle as I write this (*with* you, of course, not *at* you), because I once said the same thing.

Wrong! Let me give you the bad news first. Running a business takes time and effort; at least 25-40 hours a week once you are established and perhaps as much as 60 hours a week during that very critical first year when you are starting out. You will be spending a great deal of your day running your business: answering and returning phone calls, planning your classes and writing lesson plans, keeping your books, designing and implementing your advertisement and marketing, and so on. Although you will have time to train, you are going to have to find that time within the busy schedule that running a martial arts school inherently requires.

The good news is that perhaps for the first time in your life, you will be working for yourself, doing what you love to do, and every single extra minute that you spend productively working in your business will pay off in dividends by putting money in your pocket. That sounds kind of nice, doesn't it? It is – very nice indeed. And I wish you all the success in the world as you pursue your dreams; read on, I will give you the information you need to make it happen.

Important Point: *There is no free lunch; you are going to have to work to succeed.*

In the next Chapter, we'll get into the nuts and bolts of starting your business, which begins with choosing your advisors and mentors. The people you choose at this critical stage to assist you in making vital business decisions can make or break you in your business venture. We'll discuss how to choose them wisely and how to recognize someone who can help you reach your goals, versus a con artist who just wants to get their hands on your wallet.

THREE

SEEK OUT ADVICE FROM THE RIGHT PEOPLE

You Need a Mentor

One of the most difficult tasks you'll have to tackle when starting your new business is finding and choosing a mentor. However, choosing a mentor is one of the most important things you can do to ensure your success as a small business owner. Let me qualify that statement by saying that choosing the *right* mentor is one of the most important things you'll do to ensure your success. Choosing the wrong one can ruin you.

A mentor is the person you'll go to most often to ask questions about business and to bounce new ideas off of. In addition, your mentor can be a source of encouragement when times get tough. A good mentor will help you avoid the various pitfalls involved in starting and running your dojo, and they will point you in the right direction when you get turned around. Your mentor is kind of like your big brother or sister; he or she is always looking out for you, and is not afraid to tell you when you're screwing up.

Take your time when choosing your mentor. There will be LOTS of people who are willing to give you advice; however, much of it will be BAD advice!

Case In Point #1:

Shortly after my wife and I got married, she started working full-time with me in the office at our studio. In order to make things easier on her, I decided to farm out our billing again. We chose a billing company that had been recommended by several school owners I knew. Not only did they come with stellar recommendations; their CEO was known for building big schools in a very short period of time. We began using all of their business systems in our studio, throwing out the bulk of the systems I had developed through trial and error over the five years or so that I had been in business.

Before long, however, we started questioning the sales tactics this company promoted in their materials and seminars. Much of their approach seemed revolve around misleading the client in some fashion to justify up-selling and over-charging them. We also began to notice that the company staff spent most of their time with school owners that were in their "Gold Club" or above; if you were under $10,000 a month in gross tuition collections, you probably were not going to get a whole lot of face-time with them.

In the three years we were with them, I took a lot of bad advice from them that ended up costing me business and $$$. In addition, I lost a great deal of trust with my established students by using their crooked tactics. In the end, we ended up dropping them and ditching their systems for the old, honest, common sense methods I had always used.

Be Sure to Consult the Right Person

In addition, while a person may be an expert on some issues, there are probably some questions (like legal and tax questions) that should be referred to a specialist in that area.

Case In Point #2:

When I first began planning to open my school, I had a friend who had built a business from scratch that grossed almost $1 million per year at its zenith. Because I trusted this person I asked for her advice on a regular basis regarding business issues, and received mostly sound advice. However, when I opened my dojo I made the mistake of asking for advice on how to pay my taxes, on a quarterly basis, or at year's end (hey, I was only twenty-three years old at the time).

She advised me that there was no need for me to start paying quarterly taxes, since in her estimate I would have so many write-offs from my first-year expenditures in opening my dojo, I probably wouldn't owe any taxes at the end of the year. Needless to say, at the year's end I owed thousands of dollars in taxes and ended up paying exorbitant amounts of money in late fees and interest over the course of the next several years while I paid off the amount I owed. This one stupid mistake very nearly cost me my business.

In hindsight, I should have taken my questions to an accountant, or at the very least done some research into tax laws and taxation of business entities before following her advice. I promptly started consulting with and having my taxes reviewed by a CPA, and a few years later, I did in fact hire an extremely competent accountant that still handles my taxes to this day.

Bottom line? Be sure to refer your questions to someone who knows what they are talking about, and always research the facts regarding a decision before going on someone else's advice.

The Seven Qualities of a Good Mentor

So how do you choose the right mentor? Try to find someone that has the following seven qualities, in abundance:

- **HONEST** – A good mentor is an honest person. They will not lie or mislead others for their own personal gain. Be sure that the person you are taking advice from is a person of integrity.
- **EXPERIENCED** – A good mentor has "been there, done that." You want to find someone who has already been where you are going. This allows you to learn from *their* mistakes instead of making your own.
- **BENEVOLENT** – A good mentor sincerely cares for the welfare of others. He or she should also have a *personal* interest in you and your success. Find a mentor who likes helping others succeed.
- **ENTREPRENEURIAL** – The best mentor you can find is one with an entrepreneurial spirit, one that loves being in business. It would be preferable if it were someone who was a martial arts school owner, but this is not critical. Remember, any person you know who has built a service-oriented business from the ground up will be able to give you a ton of good advice on starting and growing your business.
- **A TRACK RECORD OF SUCCESS** – The reason why you are picking a mentor is so you can use a success concept that some business experts call "patterning." You want to pattern your success on the success of your mentor. As a successful school-owner I

know of is fond of saying, "You can't give someone something that you don't already have." Find a person who has already reached the heights to which you aspire, and they will be able to show you the quickest way to the top.

- **NO CONFLICT OF INTEREST** – This is common sense, but as one of my fellow instructors says, "If sense were common, there'd be no stupid people in the world." I can't emphasize this one enough; *don't pick a mentor that has any financial connection to your business!* You want your mentor to be totally un-biased when they are giving you business advice.

- **LIKE-MINDED** – Finally, and perhaps most importantly, your mentor should share your vision of what a successful studio should be like. If you want to run a highly profitable 200-student school, it is not going to help you much to take advice from someone who thinks that a 200-student school is a failure. Find someone that thinks like you do and who agrees with your vision.

Finding Your Yoda

Okay, my young padawan learner, I know what you are thinking. You now know the importance of having a mentor, but where will you find this mysterious master of the business arts? Never fear, the force is with you!

The fact is that you may already know someone who can help you in this regard, but you just don't realize it. I am sure there is someone in your immediate circle of influence that has at least some experience in running a small business. However, this person is not just going to jump out of the bushes one day and volunteer to become your mentor. You are going to have to do some hunting and searching, building relationships and contacts along the way that may yield a good mentor later on down the road. This is what is commonly known in business circles as *networking*.

Networking is a powerful tool that can do more for you than help you find a mentor. In fact, it is one of the most important skills you must acquire to build your business. We are going to explore the concept of networking in greater detail later on when we cover marketing and public relations, but for right now, know that it is the most likely means by which will find a good mentor.

Please note that networking is about *building relationships*. If you just walk up to someone you don't really know and begin pumping them with questions about starting a martial arts studio, you will probably put them off and lose a good potential contact. So, when you first approach a new business contact be courteous, respect their time, and have a genuine interest in who they are and what they have to tell you, even if it doesn't pertain to your immediate situation.

Also, make a sincere effort to present a professional appearance. If you are going to attend a business function where there is a strong likelihood of meeting business professionals, be sure to dress appropriately. Although it is a little dated, I recommend that you read John T. Molloy's *Dress For Success* to assist you with your professional image. Lastly, get some nice looking business cards in a heavier linen or parchment stock printed with your name, business address, and phone number, so you can easily exchange contact information with the people you are networking with.

Important Point: *You are your image. Make an impression by looking your best.*

Places To Look For a Mentor

- **Martial arts events** are great places to network.

Tournaments and seminars can present an excellent opportunity for building relationships with fellow instructors and school owners who share your business philosophy and desire to succeed.

- **Local Chamber of Commerce functions** are some of the best places to network, and that's not just for gleaning good business advice from fellow business owners. You can actually get a lot of referral business just by being active in your local chamber.
- **Industry association events** also present good networking opportunities. Attending these functions is worth the cost, if just for the contacts you will make at them. Just be sure to turn on your B.S. detector when attending the mini-seminars and presentations; like I said in the prologue, the presenters are not always acting in your best interests, and are often there just to promote their own (or their buddy's) products and services. Some of the information you get in these presentations will be useful, but *caveat emptor* is the rule of the day at these events.
- **The Small Business Administration** has a number of programs to assist the budding entrepreneur, and I strongly suggest that you take advantage of them. One of their best programs is SCORE, a non-profit organization consisting of thousands of retired business owners and executives who volunteer to counsel small business owners. Obviously, this is a GREAT place to find a business mentor. And, it's *free*. I like "free," because when you are in business for yourself, your mantra should be "free is good, free is good, free is good..."
- **One-on-one business coaching** is another option, albeit a costlier one. In a few pages I'll let you know how you can get one-on-one coaching with me if you so desire.

However, if you're interested in getting one-on-one business coaching with me I suggest you read this book cover-to-cover first. That's so you don't waste precious time during your coaching sessions asking questions that I've already answered in these pages.

One Last Thought on Mentors...

One thing I realize as I look back over my 20-year career as a professional martial arts instructor and school owner is that I didn't just have one mentor; I've had dozens. I believe that this was one of the keys to my success, as well as the fact that I am highly teachable. I didn't have a business degree or an entrepreneurial background when I started out, but I listened to what those with more experience and knowledge had to say, and then took their advice to the lab and put it to the test in my everyday business practice.

Like we used to say back in Missouri, "I'm from the Show-me State, so *show me.*" Take my advice and find a good mentor before you start, and then learn all you can from them; let them show you how to succeed. Following in the footsteps of someone who has already cut a clear trail is a whole lot easier than beating your own path to success.

Should You Use A Consultation Company?

Although I did spend a considerable amount of text and time blasting the martial arts consulting companies earlier in the book, you should know that I don't think they're all bad. I do, however, strongly discourage you from using a consulting company as your martial arts billing company. I think I already explained my reasons for this, but let me say this again for those of you who missed it the first time: there is a definite conflict of interest on the part of any martial arts billing company that offers consultation services to their clientele, and it should be obvious to you that this arrangement will not work in your favor.

Let me warn you, you are going to have a ton of people that will approach you singing the praises of their martial arts billing company's consulting services. These same people are either misled, delusional, or they are about to offer you some great oceanfront property in central Kansas. Don't listen to them.

Instead, my recommendation is that you create a stand-alone consulting company, and handle your own billing in-house (more on this in Chapter 9). Take my word for it and I can almost guarantee you won't be sorry you took my advice on this.

Important Point: *Don't use a billing company that insists on giving you business advice.*

Specifically regarding the question of whether or not you should use a consultation company; I say, "yes you should," but you need to be careful not to take everything they tell you as the gospel truth. *Avoid getting sucked into the herd mentality.* Question everything they tell you, and before you implement any new programs or marketing ideas they throw at you, examine in great detail which party will really profit from it.

Important Point: *Use a consulting company, but don't let them use you.*

Consulting companies can be a source of fresh new ideas for lesson plans, drills and activities, marketing ideas, and business practices; however, some of them (usually the ones who offer consultation services in conjunction with tuition billing) give less than stellar advice to school owners and instructors, so be careful! Implementing unethical business systems and unseemly programs in your studio can ruin your reputation in your community and destroy the respect you have gained from your clientele. Remember that "all that glitters isn't gold" and that you are ultimately responsible for your own success or failure, so choose wisely if and when you do decide on a martial arts consulting company.

An Alternative to Following the Herd

Within a year or so of releasing this book, I began receiving requests for business coaching from people who had purchased and read the Small Dojo Big Profits manual. At first, I was resistant to the idea of providing coaching for profit, and gave advice for free when and where it was requested.

Soon however, I realized two things:

1. Anything given for free is never valued.
2. I was spending a lot of time coaching people for free who didn't respect my time or my advice.

Having learned my lesson the hard way once again, I started offering one-on-one business coaching as well as more affordable online coaching via my business coaching website, MartialArtSchool-Alliance.com. While my one-on-one coaching services are no more than what you might pay for time with a good attorney or tax accountant (in my experience, considerably less actually), the coaching website is often the more attractive of the two options due to the very affordable monthly investment to join.

The upside to my coaching programs is obviously the fact that I am totally unbiased. Or as we say in Texas, "I don't have a dog in that hunt." I don't have a stake in any billing companies or equipment vendor outlets, so I am going to tell you the truth as I see it about what you need to do to be successful from a neutral standpoint.

Interested? Find out more at MartialArtSchoolAlliance.com

What's Next?

Now, on to Chapter 4: "Financing, the Old-Fashioned Way", where we will discuss how you can start your school using very little if any out-of-pocket money for start-up costs. I will outline the exact methods that I used to start my own studio when I had no money and no credit to speak of, and then I will outline a few methods that have worked for other entrepreneurs in starting their businesses.

FOUR

FINANCING YOUR SCHOOL, THE OLD-FASHIONED WAY

Neither a Lender nor Borrower Be...

We all know the old saying: "It takes money to make money." This is perhaps the most discouraging thing that you can tell a budding entrepreneur, especially if they are in the same boat that I was when I first started; broke, living on a near minimum wage salary, and with no credit to speak of. However, don't be discouraged if you are in a similar situation yourself, because with a little ingenuity and a lot of hard work (well, you didn't think it was going to be easy, did you?) you can open a studio regardless of your financial situation. Just use the same methods I used when I successfully financed my studio and you'll soon have a martial arts studio that you can call your own.

On the other hand, if you are in a favorable financial position and have lots of money to allocate toward starting your studio, or even if you have a spotless credit rating and a banker for a brother, I am still going to ask you to be open-minded and listen to what I have to say in this chapter. This information is perhaps going to be of even more benefit to you, because in the world of business it is always better to avoid risking what you have already gained, and to avoid financial risk whenever possible.

I am going to show you how to raise your own starting capital and make your new business "self-funding". Yes, if you have great credit and know the right people, you can go out and borrow money to get your business started. Yet, I am strongly of the opinion that this only adds more risk to the start-up process.

Heaven forbid should you borrow money and your school flops, you are going to be in a world of hurt. And, if you do make it big you are still going to have to make those loan payments every month, which is going to cut into your profit margins considerably. The "Small Dojo Big Profits" philosophy is based on being lean and mean, not fat and wasteful. I ask you: why create more expenses for yourself if you don't have to?

Important Point: *When funding your business, don't risk any money that you can't financially or psychologically afford to lose.*

Making Your Dojo "Self-Funding"

The method I am about to show you to finance your dojo is as time-tested as they come. I would estimate that the great majority of successful school owners in the U.S. got started using these very same methods. However, this plan is not for the lazy or weak-willed. You are going to have to steel yourself for the possibility that your first attempts at getting started may not pan out, and you will most likely end up right back at square one at least once before you get off the ground. In fact, I failed three times before I met with success using this method (this was mostly due to choosing the wrong communities to start teaching in – more on this later in Chapter 6). Yet, this method is perhaps the safest and most profitable means of starting your own studio.

Using Part-time Classes to Leverage Yourself into Fulltime Teaching

The way that I got off the ground and into my studio was by starting several part-time classes in the very community that I wanted to open my dojo in, and parlaying those classes into a full-time business. The advantages of using this method are obvious. You are building a substantial clientele before you even open the doors to your studio, the majority of whom will likely follow you when you move your classes into a full-time location. Additionally, your part-time classes will allow you a lot of financial breathing room that you wouldn't have had if you had used your own savings or borrowed money to get started on.

I know it sounds simple, but there is definitely more to doing this than meets the eye. There are several critical steps involved in going from teaching at a part-time location to owning a full-time studio, and each one deserves a considerable amount of time and attention before you move on to the next step. Follow them unerringly, however, and you will be in your own studio within a relatively short period of time.

Step #1: Choosing the Community in Which You are Going to Teach

This is perhaps the most crucial step of all. As I said before, I failed three times before I got things right, and that was mainly due to picking the wrong communities to get started in. I am going to go into greater detail in Chapter 6 on this topic, but for starters I will tell you that you should look for a community that has a **high population density**, a **high median income**, and **lots of kids** (or adults with disposable income, or women, or whatever your target market is). This is not something that you should just guess at; in Chapter 6 I will show you how to use demographics to take the guesswork out of choosing your area.

My First Big Mistake

The first big mistake I made when got started as a martial arts instructor was not spending enough time researching where I should locate my classes. Instead of using demographic information and just plain common sense to determine the most desirable location for my school, I simply started teaching at the first place that told me I could use their facilities. This turned out to be a big mistake.

First off, the town I started my classes in was known as a retirement community, which was definitely not my target clientele since I was teaching hard Japanese and Korean martial arts. It was very small and isolated as well, which meant that I would have a limited number of residents to market my services to. Despite the fact that I had zero competition in this area, my classes never really filled up enough to justify my opening a studio there. I ended up "wasting" many months teaching in that area before my job forced me to shut down my classes (this wasn't really a waste, since I learned a lot from the experience, but it would have been nice to get things right without having to go through all that).

Thankfully, the next time around I knew more about choosing a good location, and applied that knowledge to ensure my success. My next attempt worked out wonderfully, and I was able to open a full-time location within one year of teaching my first class in that area.

Important Point: *Choose a place to teach that has plenty of likely customers.*

Step #2: Finding Great Places to Teach Part-time Classes

This step is probably going to require a lot of footwork and patience. Don't be fooled into believing that just because you are a black belt, people are going to be clamoring to let you teach in their location. You are probably going to have to knock on a lot of doors and speak to a lot of people before you get the ideal host location to get started at. Trust me, though - it will be worth it.

The most important thing for you to accomplish in this step is to secure locations that are within a five mile radius of each other, and that are clustered around the area in which you have decided to eventually open your studio (see Chapter 6 for more details on this). Since you are unlikely to draw many students to your school from beyond a five mile radius of your location, it will be a waste of time to teach classes at locations that are not in the same geographical area that you are going to open your studio in. Stick with this plan, and you will ensure that you will have a healthy clientele when you open.

Make sure that you present a professional image before you start approaching potential host locations with offers to teach in their facility. Be sure to dress appropriately according to the host you will be visiting with; if you are going into a corporate complex, dress slacks with a long sleeve collared shirt and tie for guys or a pant suit for ladies might be a good idea; if you are going into a YMCA, a nice golf shirt and some khaki's are probably sufficient. You should also get some professional looking business cards printed so you can leave one with the decision-maker at each facility.

Always be polite and courteous when approaching the staff at a potential location. Believe it or not, the person at the front desk or the school secretary is your best friend when it comes to getting to talk to the real decision maker at the facility. Be nice, be charming, smile a lot, and be sure to remember his or her name so you can use it the next time you call or stop in. Also, be politely persistent! Chances are good that you aren't going to talk to someone or get a yes on the first go; just keep at them, calling back or stopping by every week or so, and chances are good that eventually they'll give in. However, whatever you do, don't become a pain in the neck or be rude or you'll probably ruin your chances of getting in there for good.

Plan your presentation before you meet with the decision maker at the facility. You are going to have to show them that you have more to offer than just kicks and punches. Talk about the benefits of taking martial arts, and how your classes will enrich the lives of the students you'll teach at their facility. If you can find any magazine or newspaper articles to back up your claims, all the better; bring them some nice color photocopies of any that you find and staple your business card to the top left corner of the article.

The best places to get into for tapping the kid's market will be YMCAs, community and recreation centers, and elementary or middle schools. Oh, and let's not forget daycare centers, which will often let you teach in their facilities rent-free just so they can advertise that they offer martial arts classes. Dance schools, cheerleading studios and gymnastics centers would all be last on my list, simply because they are less likely to let you teach there due to the obvious competition issue; still, it doesn't hurt to approach these places on the odd chance that they will rent you some space.

Locations of interest for building an adult clientele are health clubs and large corporate centers. Some large corporate centers will be willing contract with you to teach on-site classes to their employees. This works out nicely because you don't have to worry about collecting tuition from the students.

Universities, colleges and community education programs can also be another venue for offering your services. Teaching a "for-credit" class at a college or university can turn out to be a pretty sweet deal; you get paid directly by the university, you usually get a nice facility to train in, and you may even get some funds for equipment. You'll want to check with the kinesiology department as well as the community education or continuing education office when you visit a college campus. Be aware that though one office may turn you down, other departments might be open to having you teach for them, so thoroughly explore all possibilities on campus.

Usually, a host location will allow a martial arts instructor to use their facilities during their "off" hours, either for a flat rate or for a percentage of the instructor's gross profit, and the instructor is responsible for collecting his or her own tuition. Please note that paying a percentage of your gross is sometimes better than paying a flat rate, especially when you are first getting started.

Standard rates for a split with a host location range from 60% for you and 40% for them to 90% for you and 10% for them. Be reasonable, and be flexible when negotiating a split with a potential host. Offer an initial rate offer to them that is very favorable for you, then negotiate down to a rate that you can live with. Anything less favorable than 60/40 split should not be accepted, unless you have no other alternative location to teach in.

Once the amount that you are paying your host location is close to the rent you would be paying in a 1,500 to 2,000 sq. ft. facility of your own, you know it is time to get your own place. A note of caution here: keep your long-term plans for opening a studio to yourself when approaching potential host locations. Understandably, some types of facilities will not be as willing to let you teach in their location if they believe that you are going to become their competition someday.

I would advise you to remember that we live in an information age, where original ideas are harder and harder to come by every day.

Experience has taught me that it is often best to hold your cards close when it comes to letting others in on your plans and ideas. If asked what your long-term plans are, just smile and politely state that you haven't even gotten anywhere near the stage where you are ready to open your own facility. You won't be lying, and you'll be protecting your interests.

KEY CONCEPT: *Use part-time programs to leverage yourself into a full-time business.*

Step #3: Building Up the Enrollment In Your Part-time Programs

Now, how many of these part-time programs should you teach? The answer is *as many as you can juggle at one time.* The more classes you teach, the more money you will have to start your business, and the more students you will have when you open your studio. Just be sure that you don't over-extend yourself, and whatever you do, *don't quit your day job*, at least not yet. You still have a ways to go before you are ready to pay yourself a salary from your business income.

In fact, at this stage and for some time in the future you should either be re-investing all of your money back into your fledgling business (for advertising, equipment, etc. – more about this shortly) or saving the money you bring in to use for opening a full-time location. Don't spend the profits you make from your part-time classes on yourself! Doing so is committing business suicide; a little frugality now will ensure your success at a later date.

Now, let's talk about building up your enrollment. You absolutely, positively, must advertise your classes so that you will get more students. An **established** martial arts studio should be spending ten percent of their gross income every month on advertising; at this stage, however, you will probably be spending fifty percent or more of your gross on advertising.

For starters, get your website up and running, and spend some money on getting a clean design that includes a lead capture form and good search engine optimization. Your website is where all your other marketing will point to, and these days it's also where you make your first impression with a potential client. Get a good domain name, too – something short that has your town name and keywords in it (".com" domains are best). Remember, spending money on your website is really a long-term investment in your school's future, so don't skimp here.

I also recommend that you start running a weekly ad in the local family magazines, if you can afford it. In some larger metropolitan areas, this may not be feasible unless they publish a separate edition for your area; the rates will probably be too high for you to advertise in the citywide edition. If this is the case, do not be deterred; there are plenty of smaller weekly publications that you can advertise in. Look for periodicals that cater to family life and parenting, as well as those that have a wide readership among the twenty-five to thirty-five year old crowd. However, I don't recommend that you advertise in the thrift shopping papers, but you may try it for a month to see how it works.

Direct mail is another option, but it has to be done right. You need to make sure that you are targeting homes within a three to five mile radius of where you are teaching. This is your target audience, so there is no sense in paying for targeted advertisement that isn't going to them specifically. Find a company that offers good rates and that can help you put together an eye-catching mailing piece. You may try using the monthly coupon mailer services as well, as I have had some success in using them in the past. They tend to be hit or miss, so don't commit to any long-term contracts; test the waters first before you commit to more than a month or so to get a reduced rate (and that goes for all your paid advertising as well).

One absolute must is to get a listing in the local online directories.

The main directory you need to make sure you are listed in is the Google business listings (currently they call it "Google+ Business", but the name seems to change every few years). And by all means, only list a number that you are going to use for a long time! If you have to, get a cell phone and list the cell phone number in the ad, or get a business line local to the area you will open your school in, using one of the digital phone services. Later, you can then transfer that phone number to your school when you open.

This is just the tip of the iceberg when it comes to marketing and promoting your business. For more marketing ideas to build your classes, read Chapter 10: "Marketing on a Budget."

Step #4: Determine When You Are Ready to Open Your Studio

It is incredibly important that you do not open your studio until you are absolutely ready. Open too soon and you may not be able to cover all your monthly overhead expenses while still paying yourself a salary. You might even end up opening your studio while still working a day job; I would advise you to do so unless after paying all of your expenses at your studio each month you can cover your personal living expenses and maintain your current standard of living. *No matter what, however, do not go out looking for a full-time location until your current gross tuition collections exceed your projected monthly expenses by at least 25%.* This may seem excessive, but it is better to be safe than sorry. Refer to Chapter 7 for determining your projected monthly expenses.

Of course, the most desirable situation is to open at the stage when all of your monthly overhead costs are covered by your current tuition collections, including whatever monthly salary you plan to pay yourself. However, when you reach this point make sure that you allow for a percentage of your current students who will not follow you to your studio when you open. If you handle the transition properly, however, the number of dropouts should be negligible.

How I Made Ends Meet Early On

I worked a full-time job during nights and weekends while I was building my clientele up. In addition, I taught several off-site classes at daycare centers, the city community center, and the local university, and kept it up long after I opened my doors. Although this was not the ideal situation, I knew that I had to hustle to keep my doors open and pay my bills each month, so I did what was necessary to do just that.

In the long run, continuing to teach the off-site classes was probably one of the best things I ever did. I was able to get exposure for my services that I never would have received had I just stuck to teaching classes at my studio. I also made several great business contacts that continued to bring me referrals for years after I stopped teaching those classes. I highly recommend that you keep some off-site classes going, even after your school is open.

Step #5: Converting Your Part-time Students to Studio Members

Here's how you should handle this critical time to ensure that a maximum number of your current students make the transition over to the new studio:

For a seamless transition:

- A few months before you will be ready to make the move, inform the students that you are actively searching for a full-time location. Then, start talking to your students about how much better things will be when the class has their own studio. You want them to share your dream, so be specific and truthful in painting a picture of what it will be like when you open your studio. Talk to them about the benefits they will receive, such as a more flexible and expanded class schedule, having more room to train, training in nicer facilities, having more and better equipment, and so on.

- A couple of weeks before you move hold a "Pre-Grand Opening Party" just for your students and their families. Let everyone know in advance that you will be pre-enrolling for memberships to the new studio at the party. If possible, have the party at your new location as a sort of open house for your existing students.

- During the party, thank everyone for their support in helping you realize your dream of opening a martial arts studio. Then, remind everyone that you are offering a reduced rate to all your current students that will not be offered to new students, and let them know that this rate is only good if they enroll by a certain date and for a certain period of time (at least one year). Have enrollment agreements (contracts) on hand and be ready to enroll the bulk of your students at the party.

I used this exact method to enroll 100% of my existing clientele on long-term memberships when I moved my part-time classes into a full-time location. The key to making this work is in getting to know your clients and gaining their trust. That's one of the reasons why it is so important to take your time in building up your clientele before you move into a permanent location.

Understand that some of your students will be hesitant to sign an extended membership agreement. Offer them a thirty-day money back guarantee if they are not completely satisfied with the services they receive at the new facility. Also emphasize that if they wait until after your official opening date, they will pay the same rates that everyone else will pay. This should help you get the majority of your current students enrolled before you officially open your doors.

Well, there you have it, the "Small Dojo Big Profits" method to no-cost, self-funding, low-risk financing for your martial arts studio. This may not be the easiest method of getting started, but like I said before, it is a tried and true way to get your business off the ground. And, for the individual who is strapped for cash and credit-poor, it is perhaps the only way for them to get financing to open their studio.

Other Routes to Securing Financing

There are other ways to secure financing for your studio. I must warn you though, unless you can secure enough operating capital (i.e., "cash") to cover your entire operating budget for at least one year, you should stick with the method I have outlined above. Otherwise, your risk of failure will be very high, and you may not even make it past your first year in business. Additionally, unless you are confident beyond a shadow of a doubt that you will succeed in your new business venture do not borrow money from any source to start your studio.

IMPORTANT POINT: *I only recommend borrowing the start-up and operating capital for your studio if you have an extensive background and/or education in business management and entrepreneurship. Otherwise, stick with the method I have described previously in this chapter to get you going.*

If you fail to heed my advice, don't say I didn't warn you. Having said that, here is a rundown of some other methods of securing financing for your business:

- **Banks** – Bank financing is, of course, the most traditional means of getting money to start a business. Nowadays, however, most banks will not even entertain the idea of loaning money to an individual to start a small business. If, however, you have good credit and are set on using this route, I suggest going through the long and tedious process of applying for an SBA loan. Why? Because I am told that SBA lenders will finance your loan for up to thirty years, and the SBA will assist you with preparing your application. Please note that you will need a solid and well-written business plan to take to your SBA lender, so be sure to hook up with SCORE for assistance with writing it.
- **Private Investors** – Private investors are another source for financing a new business. When dealing with a private investor, however, you will often find that they charge higher interest rates and that they will not finance a loan for more than a few years. Many venture capitalists realize the *time value of money*, so they generally want to get a quick return on their money in order to flip their earnings into another investment. Your chances of finding someone who is dumb enough to loan you the money you need without evidence of a solid business plan are slim to none, so be sure to get all your ducks in a row before approaching a private investor.
- **Family and Friends** – Okay, if you want to ruin your relationships with these people fast, go ahead and borrow the money from them. Otherwise, I don't recommend it. Seriously, though, this can be a good source of financing, if you can convince them that you can make money teaching martial arts. The upside is that you are not likely

to get better terms on a loan from any other source; the downside is that if you screw up and lose their money then you have probably also ruined your relationship with whoever gave you the loan.

- **Credit Cards** – Probably the worst route to take short of borrowing the money from some guy with a thick Jersey accent named "Vinnie" that you met in a back alley. But, if you have a sufficient credit limit and an extremely favorable interest rate on your cards, this method may be more appealing to you than the other three methods I have listed above. I warn you, make sure you understand the credit terms and interest rates on your cards, as the fine print can mean the difference between being able to pay off the amount you charged and just barely being able to make the minimum payments every month.

- **Your Personal Savings and Current Income** – Even if you have some money tucked away, can cash out some stock (if you have anything left over in that 401k after the last several years), or if your current income and standard of living will allow you to finance your studio out-of-pocket, I still recommend using the "Small Dojo Big Profits" method of starting a studio. Why spend what you already have, when you can invest some sweat equity and keep your money for a rainy day?

Final Thoughts on Financing Your School

Now you know how I did it, and you understand the alternatives to using my method. No matter what route you take, *be sure to read the rest of this manual before you start.* Then you will have the "big picture" in your head, and you will be much more prepared for success than if you run off half-cocked right now and try to start your studio.

In the next chapter I am going to cover some of the legal stuff that you need to know in order to keep your tail end out of hot water. You might be tempted to just briefly skim over this chapter, but don't! Doing things the right way the first time will save you *beau coups* headaches later on down the road.

FIVE

AVOIDING LEGAL PITFALLS

First, Make Sure You Are Legal

One of the most common mistakes that a budding entrepreneur can make is failing to observe local, state, and federal requirements for legally doing business in their area. It is a simple truth that ignoring these rules, regulations, and laws can get you in serious hot water. However, you can avoid most difficulties regarding the legalities of running your own business by simply getting the right people on your team to ensure that you are observing all the pertinent laws and regulations that govern your business.

There are certain things that you need to do to be "legal" when starting your business. For instance, you will need to form some sort of business entity that you will conduct your business under, you will need to get a federal employer identification number (EIN), you may need to get a local or state business license or sales tax permit, and so forth. While I would like to be able to give you specific steps for making your business legal in your state, this book is simply not big enough to explain the myriad rules and regulations for legally doing business in each individual city and state. Hiring a good attorney and an experienced CPA will allow you to have access to valuable guidance when navigating the process of starting your business and making it legal. Do yourself a favor and find an attorney and an accountant to assist you with these matters.

Five Simple Rules for Avoiding Legal Pitfalls

The following are some simple rules that I believe every business owner should follow to help them avoid the typical legal pitfalls associated with owning a business:

Rule #1: Hire a Good Attorney and an Experienced CPA

I know, I just mentioned this. Trust me, I wouldn't repeat myself if it weren't important. If you cannot afford to hire a local attorney, you might consider using one of the so-called "legal HMO's" that have been gaining in popularity in the last few decades. Most of what you will need should be covered in a good preventative legal services policy, and the rates can't be beat (around $25 to $75 per month, depending on the plan). Considering that most attorneys charge $150 per hour and up, being able to call up a licensed attorney to bounce legal questions off of any time you like for only $25 per month is a tremendous bargain.

Another resource you might turn to for your legal needs is to purchase business legal software. I have used Quicken legal software over the last few years, and have nothing but praise for it. I have probably saved myself thousands of dollars in legal fees by using these products, but they are not a substitute for having a good attorney to turn to. Still, if you need to draft a simple legal document and don't wish to spend $500 to have it done by an attorney, these types of software products are a great help.

As I stated previously, you also need to hire an experienced CPA, because hiring an accountant in the early stages of your business will save you from potential tax headaches later on down the road. You might think you don't need an accountant, and you might be right, but why risk it? The last thing you need is the IRS breathing down your neck because you forgot to file your quarterlies. And trust me; they really don't care about hearing your excuses when you've paid your taxes late, or made mistakes on your tax return. Just hire a good accountant and be done with it; you won't be sorry if you do, but you most probably will be sorry if you don't.

Of course, the most obvious reason to hire a good accountant is that without a doubt he or she will find ways to save you money on your taxes. The tax code is extremely complex and baffling to the uninitiated, but any accountant worth their salt will be able to give you at least a half-a-dozen tax reduction strategies you can implement immediately to reduce your tax liability as a small business owner. And, I can assure you, the money you save in taxes will most likely pay for their fee many times over.

You should also purchase a good accounting software product to track your expenses and income. My accountant and I both prefer to use Peachtree's accounting software products. I suggest getting Peachtree First Accounting, both for its simple interface and the fact that it allows you to easily correct your mistakes after the fact. There is nothing worse than screwing up your books and not being able to fix it because your software is designed to prevent post-entry adjustment of figures.

Rule #2: Limit Your Liability

Okay, here's one of the main reasons that you should hire a good attorney to assist you with starting your business. Being a business owner makes you a prime target for a lawsuit, especially in our industry. You absolutely must take measures to protect your assets by limiting your personal liability in case you are sued. Simply filing a "Doing Business As" certificate with the county or state you are operating in will not be sufficient to protect your personal assets if you are sued in a court of law.

One of the most common methods that business owners can take to limit their personal liability is to select an appropriate business structure and form a separate business entity conforming to that business structure to conduct business under. This entity usually takes the form of a corporation or limited liability company, but in some instances it may be a limited partnership. All three entities act to ensure that a potential plaintiff cannot come after a business owner's personal assets in a lawsuit, but each has its own benefits and drawbacks.

It would be best if you spoke with your attorney and your CPA concerning the legal and tax benefits of each type of business entity before you decide which one you will form to operate under. Incidentally, I operated my school as a Subchapter-S corporation to avoid double-taxation, and it worked out splendidly, saving us thousands of dollars a year in taxes.

In many states, you can easily file the paperwork yourself to form a corporation or LLC. My home state of Texas even has the necessary paperwork and filing instructions for incorporation on the Secretary of State's website. For a few hundred dollars, anyone can go to the site, download the documents, and form their corporation or LLC online.

Important Tip: *Another way to protect yourself is to have each person who takes lessons from you sign a "hold harmless agreement" before they ever start training; this is an agreement that is designed to establish beforehand that the client is in good health, that they understand the dangers involved in martial arts training and that they are assuming the risk of taking classes. For minors, their parents must sign a waiver before they can participate in class. See the Appendices for an example of a hold harmless agreement/liability waiver.*

Of course, there is a great deal more to protecting your assets than just filling out some paperwork; you must also conduct your business accordingly if you expect the corporate entity to protect you should you become the target of a lawsuit. Once again, for safety's sake it is best to speak with an attorney concerning such matters.

Rule #3: Pay Your Taxes in Full and on Time

I know, this sounds like a "no-brainer", but you would be surprised at the number of people who think that they can fool the IRS and save a few hundred bucks, or that blow off paying their taxes on time. I am warning you, do not lie on your tax return and do not blow off tax deadlines! Doing so only puts you and your business at risk, and it *will* come back to haunt you. Make sure you follow all of your accountant's advice and instructions to avoid any unnecessary difficulties involving the IRS and the Treasury Department.

On a related note, if you plan to sell equipment to your students (which you should, because it's an easy added profit center – more on this in Chapter 12) you will most likely have to collect state and local sales tax. Contact your city, county and state tax offices to get more information on collecting and paying sales tax.

Rule #4: Get Insurance; GOOD Insurance

Although injury and liability insurance can be one of your larger expenses, it is well worth the cost to know that you have a sizable insurance windfall should you be sued for damages due to an injury that one of your clients or employees sustains. Although operating as a corporation or LLC will help to protect your personal assets from being subject to collection should a plaintiff win a judgment against you, your business assets are fair game. I suggest carrying a minimum of $2,000,000 in coverage, per incident, but of course you should speak with your attorney to find out what limits of coverage he or she recommends.

Although insurance rates in our industry can be higher than in related industries, you can get a very reasonable rate on a decent liability insurance policy if you shop around long enough. Although there are several specialty insurance companies that currently service the martial arts industry, obviously some offer much better rates than others, so be sure to do some comparison shopping before going with a particular company. I might also mention that some martial arts organizations have negotiated group discounts on liability insurance for their members, so check around with different organizations as to what they offer.

Rule #5: Know the Law

Before you ever start teaching your first martial arts class for profit, you need to learn about the aspects of the law that pertain specifically to the business environment. Now, I know what you are thinking: "Why hire a lawyer if I am going to have to learn this stuff myself?" Well, because you can't afford to go running to your attorney for every little question that might come up in the day-to-day operation of your studio. Even if you get a pre-paid legal coverage plan, attorneys tend to be extremely busy people, and they get irritated when they have a client that is calling them every five minutes to ask them questions. So, you'll want to save the big issues for the attorneys, and get the answers to the little questions on your own.

A good place to start is to read a book on the subject. Personally, I like the publications that Nolo Press puts out, because they are generally easy to read and understand, and they have a reputation of taking up for the little guy. I'd start with the *"Legal Guide for Starting & Running a Small Business"* by Fred Steingold.

One of the best things you can do for yourself to help ensure that you know the law as it relates to your business is to take a college course or seminar on business law and legal issues. A good place to start would be to go to the SBA's business training website. After that,

I would suggest contacting your local college or university to see what course offerings they are offering on the topic in the next few months.

It would definitely be a good idea to take a full-semester course, but you can get by with taking a seminar or a short continuing education course as well. I took an intensive five-week class on business law, and still felt that I didn't know enough about the subject. However, taking that course served its purpose, because it opened my eyes to numerous areas of my business practice where I needed to change my operating procedures to avoid potential legal problems.

When you finally decide to take a class in business law, make sure that the course you take covers, at a minimum:

- torts,
- sales and contracts,
- agency law,
- partnerships and corporations,
- employment law,
- and business regulatory law

These are the bare minimum topics that you should be aware of in operating your business. Of course, anything is better than nothing, but I want you to get your time and money's worth. Lastly, be sure to take lots of notes and ask plenty of questions about issues that you come across in your study that are specific to your business. This may be the last time you are able to get free legal advice, so take full advantage of it.

Important Point: *Spending a few hundred dollars now to get some professional assistance and advice, and taking a few hours to do some serious research into your local laws and regulations will save you a ton of headaches later on down the road.*

That should be enough information to get you started on the right foot. Remember, business laws and regulations are changing all the time, so make sure that you stay up with recent trends and changes. Always keep learning and you will be well ahead of your competition, I assure you.

Now, on to Chapter 6: "Location, Location, Location = $$$, $$$, $$$", where I'll show you how to make those dollars work for you and not against you when you choose your location.

SIX

LOCATION, LOCATION, LOCATION = $$$, $$$, $$$

So, Make Those Dollar Signs Work for You

I am sure that by now you know I am one person who definitely marches to the beat of a different drummer. I decided long ago that it was a waste of time to follow the martial arts industry crowd, since they are usually either misinformed or several years behind the curve when it comes to business information. Accordingly, you can expect that much of the information I am about to give you in this chapter is going to fly in the face of just about everything you have read on the subject in martial arts business articles and manuals.

My goal here is to show you that when you are in business bigger locations are not always better, and that this rule is especially true when it comes to being profitable in the martial arts industry. Forget what the so-called "experts" told your friend Billy Bob Black Belt at the last martial arts business convention he attended, and forget about that article you read last week in a martial arts magazine. In addition, I advise you to throw your pride to the curb, because you cannot afford to make business decisions simply for the sake of boosting your ego and having bragging rights among your friends.

I am going to tell you what worked for me when I got started, and what has worked for numerous martial arts studio owners for decades with regards to choosing the right location for a studio. Listen up, and you will save yourself a ton of money plus save yourself from suffering a lot of stress besides. If you follow my plan, when the next recession hits and all the other studio owners in town are wondering how they are going to pay the rent on their big Wal-Mart-sized vanity studios, you'll be following the "Small Dojo Big Profits" plan and laughing all the way to the bank.

Size Matters, but Not the Way You Think

I get the martial arts industry magazines every month, flip through them once and inevitably toss them in my circular file. Each month, it's the same old thing; so-and-so the martial arts magnate is being interviewed about how he or she has the largest school in their area, with "X" amount of students, "X" number of staff members, and so on.

Of course, they show pictures of this studio owner in their big huge school, wearing a tailored suit and expensive watch, and they might even have a picture of him or her standing next to their new sports car or a luxurious home in the 'burbs. I say that's all well and good, but let's talk about what they are not telling you...

The Dirty Truth

Here's the low-down; so-and-so the martial arts magnate is probably paying more than third of his monthly gross on rent, "triple nets", and his utility bill in that big huge storefront school. That's right, one-third! Those of you with a business management background know that in the mainstream business world spending thirty-three percent of your gross profits on rent and utilities would get a manager fired quicker than you can say "turn off the lights." It's sheer madness!

Just for fun and as an illustrative exercise, let's play with some conservative figures to see just how insane Mr. Magnate is for continuing to operate in his super-sized McDojo:

Rent: Let's say that Mr. Martial Arts Magnate hasn't gone totally hog wild, and has "only" leased 6,000 square feet of space for his super McDojo. Let's also say that he isn't spending too terribly much per square foot of leased space; maybe he operates in an area where the rent is much lower than the national average, or he has negotiated a "good" deal with the landlord. Even though prime real estate in most large cities and rapid-growth communities will lease for upwards of $2.00 a square foot, we'll go with a conservative figure of $1.25 per square foot:

6,000 sq. ft. times $1.25 = $7,500.00 per month base rent

"Triple Nets": Triple nets, are costs that a landlord or property management company will pass on to you when you lease in a modern high-profile shopping center. These costs are for insurance, property taxes, and common-area maintenance costs (sometimes called "C.A.M. charges"). Landlords often charge a standard persquare-footage rate for triple nets, but rarely will they charge them to their tenants according to actual costs. Although I have seen landlords charging upwards of 25% of base rent for these costs, we'll be conservative and say that Mr. Magnate is only being charged 20% of his monthly base rent:

Cost of Triple Nets = $1,500.00 per month

Utilities: Let's not forget that it costs quite a bit of money to light, heat and air condition that facility. According to E Source, "office buildings in the U.S. use an average of 17 kilowatt-hours (kWh) of electricity and 32 cubic feet of natural gas per square foot annually". In Texas, electricity costs an average of around 10.8 cents per kilowatt hour. It is easy to see that Mr. Magnate is going to be giving the utility company a hefty chunk of change each month to heat and light his super studio:

6,000 sq. ft. times 17 KWh divided by 12 months times .108 = $918.00 monthly utility costs... just for electricity!

Total Cost:

$7,500 rent + $1,500 triple nets + $918 utilities = $9,918.00 per month… or basically ten large on rent and utilities each month.

Wow, that's a lot of money to be dropping on rent and utilities each month, considering that only a small percentage of martial arts studios collect over $10,000.00 per month in gross tuition collections. Now, what do you think your chances are of keeping your doors open if you follow Mr. Magnate's lead and go out to lease a huge studio? Are you starting to see where I am coming from here?

More to Think About Before You Open: A Quick Lesson in Business Terminology

Rent is what accountants and financial analysts call a *fixed cost*. Fixed costs are a foreseeable cost, which is good; you pretty much know ahead of time what those costs are going to be so you can plan accordingly to meet them. However, it's the *variable costs* that will get you if you aren't careful. Variable costs are costs that can increase or decrease according to your sales volume and other unpredictable factors. Since you can't really know with a certainty what your variable costs will be from month to month and year-to-year, it is best to keep your fixed costs as low as possible so you can absorb a sudden increase in variable costs if necessary.

Let's say for instance that Mr. Magnate is operating just fine for a while, but then he has an unforeseen increase in his variable costs. His hot water heater breaks and floods his studio, costing him $6,000 for water damage recovery, repairs, and to replace equipment (he should have had contents insurance, but that's neither here nor there). Suddenly, he is in a world of hurt because guess where that $6,000 is going to come from?

You guessed it, his salary! Now, if Mr. Magnate is living the lifestyle that we are led to believe he lives; nice house, sports car, expensive clothes, etc, that $6,000 is going to hurt him in the worst way possible. Yet, if he had kept his fixed costs low and put some money away every month besides, that six-grand would just be a little speed bump in the road of life.

Success Strategy: You should always work to keep your fixed costs as low as possible; this will give you plenty of "breathing room" to pay for unforeseen costs.

It is my contention that an *acceptable* cost for a lease should be no more than 10% of your monthly gross income. Notice I said "acceptable", not "ideal." The ideal cost for anything in your business is as cheap as you can get it. So, if you can find a cherry space that's located right in the middle of your target area for 50 cents a square foot, jump on it.

Success Strategy: *According to the "Small Dojo Big Profits" way of thinking, you should be spending no more than 10% of your projected gross profit on leasing your studio space.*

In the next chapter, "Business Plans and Budgeting," I am going to go into detail about how staying lean and mean can make the difference between staying afloat during hard times and going under. For now, I just wanted to illustrate how ridiculous it is from a business standpoint to spend that much money on your location when it is simply not necessary. Speaking of which, let's go over exactly why you don't *need* to have a studio that's the size of Rhode Island.

Making It Fit

Small studio size does not necessarily have to mean a small enrollment. With efficient studio layout and class scheduling, you can
easily accommodate 240+ students in a 1,500 – 2,000 sq. ft. studio.
That's right, 240 students or more can be serviced in a studio that's
not much bigger than the average starter home.

On the following page, let's take a look at an example of a small
studio floor plan where the owner has made the most of the available
space.

**Example of Floor Plan for a 1,500 Square Foot
Studio:**

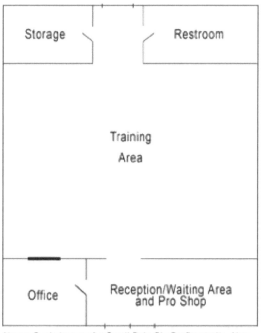

Above: Basic layout of a Small Dojo Big Profits studio. Note
the lack of changing rooms and showers. With proper class
scheduling you easily can accomodate ten students for every
100 square feet of space. Be sure to allot at least 1,000 square
feet for your training area when planning your facility.

As you can see, every inch of space has been utilized to the greatest efficiency, with no wasted space. Having a separate, walled-off viewing area for spectators will cut down on the noise level during class, yet it enables parents, family members, and potential students to observe the quality of instruction in the classes. In addition, the office is located near the front of the school, so the office personnel may easily greet incoming students and potential clients.

While 1,000 square feet of training area may not be a huge classroom, it is sufficient to hold class for up to 20 students or more at one time, if the instructor knows how to structure their classes correctly. While having the restroom and changing area located in the back of the school necessitates having strict and posted policies to limit spectator access to the studio training area, this will save you a lot of headaches and liability. Overall, however, this is an efficient and effective studio layout.

Efficient Class Scheduling is the Key

The real key to making such a location work is efficient class scheduling. Efficient class scheduling will allow you to service a great number of students in a relatively small studio space. In other words, having an efficient and effective class schedule allows you to stay "lean and mean" in your studio operation.

In addition, an efficiently planned schedule provides you with a great deal of flexibility in case of a rapid influx of students. Many school owners, when facing the rather desirable challenge of experiencing a rapid growth in their enrollment, immediately start thinking "bigger studio." This kind of knee-jerk reactive thinking is detrimental to your business, because the increased overhead won't leave you any cushion if things go the opposite direction. Instead of expanding your location when you get more students, you should simply expand your class schedule.

When planning your schedule, consider that your target for attendance is about 15-25 students attending each class twice per week. You should also have a Monday/Wednesday and a Tuesday/Thursday schedule for your "main" classes, with ancillary classes like sparring and special clubs on Fridays. If you teach six classes per night on Monday through Thursday, and each student attends class twice a week during these four nights, you can easily accommodate 240 students in your small studio with this type of schedule, an example of which I have included on the following page.

Class Time	Mon.	Tuesday	Wed.	Thurs.	Fri.
3:30 PM	Little Dragons Ages 4-6 3:30 – 4:00	White Belts 3:30 – 4:15	Little Dragons Ages 4-6 3:30 – 4:00	White Belts 3:30 – 4:15	
3:45 PM					
4:00 PM	Break		Break		
4:15 PM	Kids Karate Class Beginners Ages 7-12 4:15 – 5:00	Kids Karate Class Intermediate Ages 7-12 4:15 – 5:00	Kids Karate Class Beginners Ages 7-12 4:15 – 5:00	Kids Karate Class Intermediate Ages 7-12 4:15 – 5:00	
4:30 PM					
4:45 PM					
5:00 PM	Kids Karate Class Intermediate Ages 7-12 5:00 – 5:45	Kids Karate Class Advanced Ages 7-12 5:00 – 5:45	Kids Karate Class Intermediate Ages 7-12 5:00 – 5:45	Kids Karate Class Advanced Ages 7-12 5:00 – 5:45	
5:15 PM					
5:30 PM					Kid's Sparring Class 5:30 – 6:15 PM
5:45 PM	Kids Karate Class Advanced Ages 7-12 5:45 – 6:30	Break	Kids Karate Class Advanced Ages 7-12 5:45 – 6:30	Break	
6:00 PM		Little Dragons Ages 4-6 6:00 – 6:30		Little Dragons Ages 4-6 6:00 – 6:30	
6:15 PM					Special Clubs 6:15 – 7:00 PM
6:30 PM	White Belts 6:30 – 7:15	Kids Karate Class Beginners Ages 7-12 6:30 – 7:15	White Belts 6:30 – 7:15	Kids Karate Class Beginners Ages 7-12 6:30 – 7:15	
6:45 PM					
7:00 PM					Adult Sparring 7:00 – 7:45 PM
7:15 PM	Break	Break	Break	Break	
7:30 PM					
7:45 PM	Teen and Adult Karate Class 7:30 – 8:30 PM	Teen and Adult Karate Class 7:30 – 8:30 PM	Teen and Adult Karate Class 7:30 – 8:30 PM	Teen and Adult Karate Class 7:30 – 8:30 PM	
8:00 PM					
8:15 PM					
8:30 PM					

Of course, this schedule is just an example, but it is very close to the one I used for a number of years in my own studio. This schedule allowed us to keep our classes small enough to give good instruction and individual attention to each student, even during the "back-to-school rush" of August to November when we would enroll the majority of our new students. You should adopt something similar to use in your own studio when you open, but be ready to adjust the times to accommodate for local school schedules and so forth.

Success Strategy: To accommodate more students, expand your class schedule.

By the way, take a good look at how the schedule is set up to allow the younger students (ages 4-12) to attend either in the early afternoon or later in the evening hours. This "early/late" schedule for the kid's classes is something that a lot of schools don't do, but they should, since the majority of the students in most martial arts studios are under the age of twelve. Busy parents love convenience and flexibility, and having a schedule like this one can be a big selling point when discussing enrollment with the parents of new students.

Important Point: People will pay a premium for convenience.

Money Talks

The economic advantages of operating in such a small location are obvious; one-fourth the rent and overhead of the 6,000 square foot "super-studio", yet with the ability to service a sufficient number of clients to reap a tidy profit. I don't want to go into hard numbers *yet*, but let's just throw some rough numbers up on the wall and see how they stick:

240 students at $99 per month base tuition = $23,760 gross tuition collections per month...

Man, I really like the sound of that. I'd like to point out the fact that this figure doesn't include testing fees, Pro Shop Sales, special events, or other additional profit centers. Still, let's just assume that twenty-four grand is all you gross each month. Using the same benchmark figures that we used for Mr. Magnates *uber*-dojo, but calculating the costs at 1,500 square feet instead of 6,000:

- 1,500 sq. ft. times $1.25 = $1,875 per month rent
- $1,875 times .20 = $375.00 in triple nets per month
- 1,500 times $1.35 divided by 12 = $168.75 per month utility costs
- Total Cost in Rent and Utilities = $2,418.75

Or, you'll be spending roughly ten percent of your gross tuition collections on rent and utilities. This figure, as I said, does not take into account income from other profit centers. If we round up that $24,000 per month to say, $28,000 to account for income from those other profit centers, we can see that $2,418.75 is well within our acceptable budget for rent (and utility costs). Now, those numbers make good business sense, and even if you won't have bragging rights to having the largest dojo in town, you can have bragging rights to having the highest profit margin in town. Which would you rather have?

Where Should You Locate Your Studio?

This question probably deserves more attention than any other in this book. The old cliché of "location, location, location" is certainly fitting when it comes to choosing where to put your martial arts studio, but not necessarily in the traditional understanding of the adage. Most people think that having a "good location" for a studio means locating in a high-foot-traffic area. While I agree that having lots of foot traffic outside your door does help with building your enrollment, I really don't think that it is *necessary* for filling up your classes. Besides, the cost of leasing such a location is often not worth the foot traffic you will get for it.

The most important consideration in choosing where to locate your studio is its proximity to potential students. Let me say that again: your studio must be located near your client base; it's as simple as that. Without fulfilling this one important requirement for choosing a location, your school will fail. No matter how nice your facility is, if you don't have a sufficient number of *quality* potential customers in a 3-5 mile radius of your studio to fill it, chances are good that you never will.

Notice also that I said "quality" potential customers; just having people around who you think might want to take your classes isn't quite good enough to ensure your success. You want to be in an area where you will attract the right clients, ones that have sufficient expendable income to afford your services and enough spare time to attend your classes. This requires some foresight and planning on your part, because first you must decide what type of student you will cater your services to.

Success Strategy: Locate your studio in an area where there are lots of quality prospects who would be likely to take advantage of your services.

Here is a point that deserves careful consideration: I recommend that you find a niche and stick with it. I can tell you from experience, and a lot of instructors out there will agree with me; trying to be all things to all people is a surefire path to mediocrity and eventual failure in business. You are not Amazon.com; you don't have their resources and you therefore you can't expect to do business as a large corporation does.

In fact, in this Information Age economy, fortunes are made (and lost) on a business' ability to find niche markets and focus their products and services on catering to those markets. Due to the constant introduction of new technologies, focusing on a market niche and specializing in a particular area of commerce has become increasingly important to a company's ability to succeed. Just think of any company that has made a name for itself in the last twenty years, and I guarantee you will find they gained their success by specializing in and catering to niche markets.

Let's examine just what this means to you, and how this concept figures in to your choosing a location.

Choosing a Niche Market

It's time to address the issue of choosing your market niche, a.k.a. your target market. From the outside, finding a target market seems like a relatively simple process. You just figure out who wants what you have and market your products and services to them, right?

Wrong! Remember martial arts myth #2? Just because you have a product or service to sell it doesn't necessarily mean that people want to purchase that product. I hate to burst your bubble, but the martial arts industry is just like any other industry and it follows the same laws and rules of doing business. And, one of the most important rules to remember for your business success is that ***market demand dictates production.***

What this means is that no matter how good you think your product or service is, if people don't want it or need it, they aren't going to buy it, period. While it is quite possible that you will be able to find a target market that will happily purchase your current programs, be aware that *it may be necessary for you to change the way you present and market your services.* You might even have to change the focus of what you offer, or move to an area where there are people who are willing and eager to pay for what you teach. However, if you want to be successful, such sacrifices are part and parcel of playing the game to win.

Success Strategy: If you want to succeed, offer a service that people want.

Making the decision as to what market niche you are going to go after deserves careful attention to several factors: your personal preferences as to what type of student you would prefer to have; what your own personal strengths are and what your area of expertise is; and whether there are any under-served market niches in your immediate area. All of these factors are important, but that last one deserves careful attention, because it could make you an instant success. If you can recognize and capitalize on a sector of the market whose needs are not being met by existing businesses, you can pretty much write your own ticket. Therefore, do your market research and carefully consider your options as to what sector of the market you are going to go after before you write your business plan and start your business.

Success Strategy: Find an unmet need in the market, and create products and services to fulfill that need.

Finding People Who Want What You Have

So how do you figure out if people are going to want what you have to offer? Well, look around and see if there is a market for it. For example, look at the market for kid's martial arts programs. If you have read any of the martial arts industry magazines over the last few decades, you have probably read somewhere that most studios teach, on average, about 70% children. This is a fairly good indication, at least at first glance, that there is a market out there for children's classes.

Now, this is great if you want to teach kids, but what if the martial art you plan to teach isn't well-suited to children, or you just plain hate being around rug rats? That just leaves the adult market. So, how can we find out what the potential for the adult market is? Let's look at an expert from outside of our industry to get an answer.

Author and economist Paul Zane Pilzer believes that the wellness industry is where the next group of millionaires will be made in our country and around the world. He is so convinced of this premise that he wrote a book entitled "The Wellness Revolution," in which he outlines in great detail just why he believes the wellness industry is on the rise. Among his reasons, he cites the ubiquity of the aging baby-boomer generation, who are currently responsible for a huge chunk of the $200 billion-plus that is generated each year in wellness related purchases and expenditures in our economy. This figure includes money spent on health club memberships, fitness classes and fitness equipment, as well as other expenditures such as for nutritional supplements, diet books, and so forth.

Now, do you think that there is a market niche to be found within the wellness industry for your martial arts classes? You bet there is! People get bored with gym memberships and workout videos, and are constantly looking for new ways to exercise and stay in shape. Market your martial arts programs properly, and you could end up attracting many of these disgruntled wellness-seekers into your studio.

Do you see where I am going with this? Martial arts for self-defense, fitness, children, the aging population, etcetera; these are all possible niche markets for you to tap into. Now, how does this exactly fit into your choosing a location for your studio? Surely you remember the three-to-five mile rule? Because most people want convenience and accessibility in the products and services they purchase on a regular basis, you need to locate your studio where clients in your niche are! Knowing this, we can surmise that opening a martial arts studio specializing in teaching super-high-speed paramilitary combat killing techniques in the middle of an area that is 90% married families with 2.5 children per household would be a great way to secure our demise. So, we must do some market research before we choose our studio location to avoid making a similar mistake.

For instance, if you like working with kids, you should open your studio in an area that has a lot of kids within a three to five mile radius of the studio. If you prefer teaching adults, you should open your studio in an area where there are a lot of young professionals in the 18 to 30 year-old age range, or where there are a lot of retirees, because these age groups traditionally have both disposable income and time to pursue activities outside of work. I could go on like this forever, but I think you get the idea.

Now, how do you figure out where your target market lives? This is going to take some work on your part, which will involve doing some reconnaissance, some research online, and just applying good-old common sense. Of course, since each geographical area is different, I can't really specifically tell you where to locate your school; this is something you are going to have to figure out on your own. However, I can give you some general guidelines to help you get pointed in the right direction, and just so you don't get stuck at this point, I am also going to give you a plan to follow that will help you in your quest of choosing the right location for your studio.

Where Are My "Peep's"?

No, not the Easter candy, the people you want to sell your services to. Let's examine two of the main niche markets that martial arts studios cater to in order to give you some idea of where to start doing your market research. Please note that much of this information is geared toward opening a school in or near a large city, but it can be adapted for doing research before opening a studio in a smaller community. Also note that there are "sub-niches" within these two major groupings, so it is up to you to fine-tune your marketing efforts to really zero in on specific sub-sections of your target market.

Children

As I said before, kids are definitely where the money is at, but not all the money. Still, they are a reliable source of income for a martial arts studio. Some good indications that there will be an adequate number of children in a particular area are:

- **Elementary and middle schools** – Look for a location where there are a minimum of two to three elementary and one to two middle schools in a three to five mile radius.
- **Proximity to housing** – A good location should be within close proximity to several neighborhood communities that are known to house a high number of nuclear families (you know, two car garage, 2.5 kids, etc.).
- **Proximity to shopping malls, department stores, large grocery stores and strip centers** – Take a hint from the fast food industry; when Burger King, Wendy's, Taco Bell, and other fast food franchises want to find a new location for their restaurants, how do you think they do their market research? I'll tell you how – they find a location within a few blocks of an existing McDonald's franchise. I know, it sounds simple, but it is an effective method. You can use the same method by looking for large-chain department and grocery stores and finding locations near them. Target, Wal Mart, Kroger's, Sav-on, and other big chains are the ones you want to look for when choosing a good location. Also, scope out their parking lots for late-model SUV's and other high-priced luxury cars. This is a good indication of the income level of the people who frequent these businesses, and it will give you an idea of the level of disposable income the residents have in that area.

Young Professionals

There are a good number of schools that are doing quite well financially by catering to the adult population, either by teaching fitness-oriented programs, self-defense and reality-based programs, or both. Young professionals are a good sub-section of this market to tap into, because most of them don't have kids yet and many aren't married. This frees up a lot of their time and income to do other things, a luxury that many married and divorced working parents don't have. So where are you going to find these people?

- **Proximity to housing and proximity to business and technology centers** – A good location should be within close proximity to upscale apartment complexes in trendy areas that cater to young professional types. While you might think that locating in the suburbs would make more sense, when it comes to young professionals that could be a mistake. Many young professionals have not yet even thought about buying a house, since they are still looking for a mate and figuring out what they want to do when they grow up (man, to have those problems again... but, I digress). They tend to live closer to where the "action" is, and subsequently prefer to live near where they work and where most of their social activities take place. Once again, look for upscale apartment developments and condominium communities in urban areas.
- **Proximity to shopping malls, department stores, large grocery stores and strip centers** – The same thing applies here that I mentioned in the last section on kids and families, but be on the lookout for hip and trendy clothing stores, or virtually any large chain businesses that cater to the younger crowd.

Using Demographical Information

A good source for getting fairly accurate demographic information to verify your initial research is the good old Census Bureau. You can also purchase demographic reports from companies that specialize in providing such information, and these demographics companies can assist you with your market research.

However, for the cost of a little time and effort you can do the same research on your own for free. Remember our mantra, "Free is good, free is good, free is good..." The only shortcoming to this method is that in larger cities you will want to get this information by zip code, which the Census Bureau reports don't have. Even so, the Census Bureau website is a good place to start.

When evaluating demographical information, you want to look at three key factors; population density, income level, and household information. Obviously, high population density areas are highly preferred over sparsely populated areas; however, this shouldn't be a problem for you if you have done your homework and chosen a location for your school in an area that has already been scouted and selected by a big retail chain.

Income level is another important factor, since you certainly want to be in a position to price your services high enough to earn a comfortable living. You would do well to remember that parents will generally spend more money on their kids than they will on themselves, so if you plan to open in an area that has a relatively low average household income, you should probably focus on providing instruction for children.

Lastly, household information is extremely important. This data will tell you about marital status, number of children, number of family members who are employed per household, and so on. Once again, this is extremely vital information; do not overlook it.

Success Strategy: Use demographic reports to find the best area in which to start your business.

Getting Down to the Brass Tacks

Okay, you've decided on a market niche, you've figured out the general area where you want to open your studio, and you've developed your part-time programs in that area so you have a built-in client base - now it's time to start looking for a space to lease. You know that you don't need anything more than 1,200 to 2,000 square feet, and that you want to keep your rent as low as possible. Now, how are you going to get the ideal space?

Well, never fear! The "Small Dojo Big Profits" method to finding the perfect location is written in explicit detail below. Let's get started finding our perfect space!

Step #1 to Finding Your Perfect Location:

First, start in the obvious places:

- First, go scout out the strip malls and shopping centers in the area.
- When you find a vacant location that looks appealing, call up the management company and inquire about the space.
- *Take notes!*
- DO NOT TELL THEM YOU ARE GOING TO OPEN A MARTIAL ARTS STUDIO, at least, not yet. Just say that you are looking for about 1,200 to 2,000 square feet of retail space and would like to know how much the space is leasing for.

- Do not start negotiating a lease at this time; you are just trying to get a feel for the going rates in your area.
- Try to get information on at least five to ten good locations at this time.
- Also, be sure to scout locations that are in upscale, midrange, and not-so-desirable locations so you have a good sense of the price ranges you are working with.

Step #2...

Next, go look in less obvious places:

- You don't just want to limit your options to strip malls and shopping centers; in fact, they are probably not likely to turn up your final choice for a location because the rent is usually too high in these centers. If you find a good deal, take it, but just not right away. Now that you have checked these places out, it is time to go out and start scouting less obvious areas.
- Grab your car keys, because you are going to do some driving. Specifically, you are going to conduct some recon near the locations you first scouted by searching in concentric circles out from these areas.
- You should be on the lookout for small business developments, smaller strip malls, office complexes, industrial warehouses (don't laugh, you can find some real gems by looking at local warehouse space), as well as stand-alone single-unit retail properties.
- Note that older business locations have a habit of being swallowed up by housing developments as cities expand and grow, so do not dismiss residential areas in your search.
- *You will find your best deals by taking the time to do this*

research, so be thorough! Even if it looks like a building is fully occupied, scout it out anyway.

- *Also, don't be shy!* Ask the current tenants if they know of any vacant space in the area, and if they plan to move anytime soon. If you don't ask, you'll never know, and you might miss a good deal because of it.

Step #3...

Once you find a likely location, investigate it thoroughly:

- *First, call up the city planning department and find out what the zoning laws are for the building location.* Be specific; give them the exact address of the location you intend to lease. Nothing could be worse than to invest a ton of time and effort into finding a great location, then signing a lease, only to find out that you are limited in the type and manner of business you can conduct there. Do not skip this step!

- *Next, hire a commercial building inspector to inspect the building.* It will cost you anywhere from $50 to $300, but it will be worth it. Make sure that they inspect the structural elements of the building, plumbing, electrical, heating and air conditioning systems. They should check for vermin, pests and for mold problems as well. Finding problems now will save you big headaches later.

- *Third, call up the local utility company and get a 12-month average of the utility bills for the location.* If the bills are too high, there could be something wrong with the heating and AC or the building may not have been built to code when it was originally constructed.

Step #4...

Consider other not-so-apparent factors:

- Number one is parking; will you have adequate parking for your clients?
- Also, think about the exterior lighting. You will most likely be teaching classes at night, and your patrons will want to feel safe when entering and leaving the studio.
- Speaking of which, is this place located in a relatively safe neighborhood? Don't lease a place in some rough part of town just because the rent was cheap.
- Is there an existing sign on the exterior of the building, or is there even space for signage?
- Does the space have adequate restroom facilities and plumbing?
- How's the lighting inside the location?
- Will you need to modify the space to make it habitable?
- How is the flooring? Is it concrete, carpet, tile, or wood?
- Will the landlord pay for improvements?
- If so, is he or she going to tack the cost on to your rent?

And so on. Once you have found the location you want and everything looks good, ***stop and assess the situation***. Now is the time to play it cool. If you go running to the landlord or property manager like a kid coming through the gates at Disney World, he or she is going to see you coming and jack you over something fierce. You need to exercise your self-control at this point, stay calm, and negotiate the best deal for the location. If you do not have experience in negotiating commercial lease space, it may be best to hire someone to negotiate the lease for you.

Using an Agent/Broker

Open up the phone book and start calling commercial leasing broker/agents. Tell them your situation and what you need. Do not be surprised if some of them refuse to represent you; your lease will likely be so small that some agent/brokers you contact will not want to bother with you due to the low commissions they will likely earn on the deal. When you find one who you feel comfortable with that is willing to represent you, tell them exactly what you want in your lease and let them do their job.

However, you must remember that this is a negotiation, so you will likely have to concede some of your demands in order to get a deal signed. So long as you get most of what you want, you are doing okay. If the landlord refuses to change his "standard lease" (which you should never, ever, ever sign without having a leasing agent and a good real estate attorney look it over first) or if he refuses to meet any of the "deal breaker" terms you are negotiating, walk away and find another space. No matter how "perfect" the space is, it's a dog if you are getting taken to the cleaners in your lease. Trust me on this, take your time and always be willing to walk away from the deal!

Checklist for Things You Should Negotiate to Include in Your Lease:

- Make sure that the rent commencement date on the lease gives you plenty of time to improve the facility before you have to start paying rent. There is no reason why you should be paying rent on a location that isn't ready to do business in.
- Make sure that your initial lease is for the shortest term possible (one or two years, tops), while retaining an exclusive right to extend the lease at the end of the initial

term. That way, if things don't go well, you can bail with no legal repercussions.

- Allowable rent increases should be kept to a bare minimum, and should be limited to a percentage of the original lease amount (to reflect inflation) when renewing the lease after the initial term.
- The lease should clearly define the terms of payment and return of the security deposit.
- You should try to get the landlord to make any improvements that you will need as part of the lease agreement.
- Get specific rights for signage and sign placement in the lease agreement.
- Permitted use is an important consideration. Make certain that you list any foreseen business usage in the lease, no matter how obscure it may seem. For instance, you might include personal training or fitness classes, daycare or after-school care, yoga, or other uses.
- Exclusivity and non-competition clauses are another issue. Make sure that the lease specifically states that the landlord will not allow any competing businesses to rent space in the same building or in an adjoining complex.
- Sub-letting clauses can sometimes turn out to be useful for the tenant later on down the road. Try to get some form of permission in the lease to sub-let your facility.
- Ensure that the lease spells out your rights and usage of parking for your business.
- Negotiate a reasonable period to "cure" a default, preferably 60 days or more.
- Try to get your CAM charges/triple nets as low as possible, and have an attorney read the fine print to make sure there are no hidden charges.
- Get provisions in the lease for the landlord's responsibility for repairing the premises in the event of

malfunction or damage. The less the number of
responsibilities you have for maintenance and repair, the
better.

- Retain your right to terminate the lease should the
landlord default in another area of the agreement. Your
attorney should be able to brief you on these rights and
tell you specifically what should be included in
your lease.
- Finally, whenever possible, try to retain your right to file
suit in case of a dispute.

As you can see, finding a good location can be a lot of work.
However, keeping your overhead down is going to be a constant
battle from here on out, so it is best if you get started on the right foot
by reducing one of your biggest expenses at the outset. The money
you'll save on rent by following these steps will be well worth the
time, effort and patience you had to expend in doing so.

Speaking of saving time and money, I will be discussing these
issues in great detail in the nest chapter. Are you ready? Then turn
the page so you can start learning how to maximize your profits
through effective business plans and budgeting.

SEVEN

BUSINESS PLANS & BUDGETING

A.K.A., Being a Cheap Son of a Gun

First, let me clarify some terminology. A ***budget*** is a projection of all the incomes you are going to have coming into your business and all the money you are going to have to spend in the course of running your business operations over a given period of time in order to stay solvent. A ***business plan*** is a **written** set of strategic steps that the leaders of a business intend to take in order to pursue success in their enterprise. ***Strategic planning*** is evaluating your business strengths and using that knowledge to take advantage of current opportunities in the market.

Of all the areas that are discussed in the martial arts business industry, business planning and budgeting probably receive the least attention. In fact, I would hazard a guess that if you have read an article on running a martial arts studio in the past year, it was about either marketing or teaching. Am I right? Well, that's no surprise; school owners definitely need to be able to attract new students and then keep those students for the long haul in order to have a stable, successful business.

Regardless of this obvious fact, I don't give a horse's behind how much money a school owner makes; if he or she doesn't manage that money well and keep close tabs on their cash flow and expenditures, they *will* fail. Maybe not right away, but it is only a matter of time until they do. No business can hemorrhage cash for an indefinite period of time without eventually suffering some serious repercussions because of it. Once again we return to the adage of ***"Fail to plan, and plan to fail."***

Since you are reading this book, I am fairly positive that you do not wish to become a statistic. Instead, I believe that you want to succeed, and in the worst way possible. If this is truly the case, and you want to be in business for the long haul, then take my advice: you absolutely, positively must be willing to learn and apply sound principles of planning and budgeting in order to survive and prosper in the new economy.

If I can sum up in a nutshell what the sound principles of good business plans and budgeting are all about, it is this: "Waste not, want not." I believe that this philosophy truly cuts right to the heart of the matter. So, cut out the waste in your business, and you will go a long way toward achieving long-term success as a martial arts school owner.

Important Point: *Careful planning will lead to success.*

Another Look at Mr. Martial Arts Magnate

To define what is wasteful and what is necessary, I think it is only proper that we should look at the differences between typical business expenditures in a large studio compared to those of a "Small Dojo Big Profits" studio. In this spirit, let's take another look at our old friend Mr. Martial Arts Magnate and his probable state of financial affairs.

Let's assume that Mr. Magnate is doing really well, and has 400 students in his super-studio, with 300 students in his main martial arts program and 100 in other programs like fitness and self-defense classes. With tuition and testing fees, and also accounting for family discounts, each regular student should be worth about $110 per month, while the others are probably worth about $50 per month.

---

300 times $110.00 = $33,000

100 times $50.00 = $5,000

Total gross in Tuition and Test Fees = $38,000 per month

Hey, that's not too shabby. Once you roll in Pro Shop Sales and special events, Mr. Magnate is probably grossing well over $40,000 a month. Sounds like a lot of money, right?

Well, not after you factor in what it costs Mr. Magnate to run that huge place. Let's do a little rundown of the expenses Mr. Magnate has in his hypothetical super-studio:

Rent – We already figured this one out in the last chapter at a conservative estimate of **$9,000** per month.

Utilities – We'll round up our last figures to about **$1,200** per month to include waste, water and sewage.

Wages and Salaries – This is where it starts to get even more interesting. What most people don't realize is that it takes a heck of a lot of additional people to maintain a studio once you get past 300 students. You have to have a full-time office manager to handle the paperwork, attend to customer service issues, and answer the phones; assistant instructors to teach extra classes and to assist the main instructor on the floor; possibly an enrollment director to teach intro lessons and keep track of setting enrollment appointments and renewals; and perhaps someone to run the Pro Shop and greet people at the door. In a smaller studio you don't need that many people to run it because there are fewer students, which equates to less work to do. Anyway, let's assume that Mr. Magnate is paying his office manager a salary of $2,000 a month, his enrollment director $3,000 a month in salary and commissions, and his assistant instructors a combined amount of $3,000 per month. Now, let's add in about an additional 15% that he has to pay for matching their tax contributions (you didn't know that employers had to do that, did you?) and you get about **$9,200** per month in salaries and wages.

Advertising – Hey, it costs some bucks to keep enough students rolling through the doors to maintain an enrollment of 400. Consider that the average for monthly student attrition in martial arts schools is about 5% a month. That means that each and every month that Mr. Magnate is open he is losing about 20 students. The reasons why could be due to someone in the family losing their job, or they moved away, or it could be due to other factors we'll discuss in Chapter 11.

Regardless, this means that Mr. Magnate has to be on his toes to make sure that he enrolls that many new students per month. Now, if he and his staff are really sharp, they can enroll 40-50% of the people who inquire about their programs into long-term memberships. That means that Mr. Magnate has to advertise enough to generate about 50 inquiries (leads) for his services each month.

Even if you are using effective paid advertising along with a combination of low-cost marketing, it is quite possible that a school owner will have a per-lead cost of about $50-$100 a lead. That means that it costs the owner $50-$100 in advertising to get one prospective customer to call his studio and inquire about enrolling. So, Mr. Magnate needs to spend about **$4,000** per month, or about 10% of his gross profits on advertising.

Insurance – Mr. Magnate has a lot to lose. He is a prime target for a lawsuit, especially with those flashy clothes and that nice car he drives. He had better have some good insurance coverage on his studio to cover his rear end. Figure that he will pay about $10.00 per student per year for liability coverage, which comes out to about **$340** a month for insurance.

Legal and Accounting Expenses – Mr. Magnate probably has an accountant do his bookkeeping, and routinely consults an attorney for legal issues. Figure another **$300.00 to $500.00** per month for both.

Office Expenses – Paper, printer ink, pens, forms, certificates and letterhead, and other office supplies add up at the end of the month, not to mention all the toilet tissue and paper towels that 400 people use in a month. Add in hiring a cleaning service to keep a 6,000 square foot studio spotless and presentable every day while 400 customers truck in and out of there, and you have an additional **$2,000 to $3,000** a month in overhead.

Repair and Maintenance – The wear and tear that 400 people place on a commercial location is amazing; torn carpet, broken tiles, chipped paint, graffiti on the walls, and stopped up commodes, in addition to HVAC filters and light bulbs. Figure **$250.00** per month.

Telephone – The lifeline of the school, don't leave home without it. Mr. Magnate also probably has a cell phone as well as internet service. Combined cost is probably **$300 to $400** per month, including long distance and such.

Miscellaneous Expenses – This includes unforeseen expenditures that come up from time to time as well as costs for travel, meals, and entertainment for training seminars and tournaments. It can also include costs for putting on special events and what not. This figure will include replacing broken and worn out training equipment. Estimate it at **$1,000** per month.

Cost of Goods Sold – Cost of equipment sold in the Pro Shop, which will be about **$2,000** per month.

Billing Company Collection Fees – What, you didn't think they collected all that money for free just because they like Mr. Magnate did you? Figure a rate of about 7% of gross tuition collections. That's quite a chunk of change, don't you think? For posterity's sake, we'll add in the cost of getting "box" kits from one of the industry associations every month to this figure: **$2,900** a month.

Okay, now it's time to add up the total for all this extravagance that Mr. Magnate insists on having in order to stroke his ego:

Expense
Monthly Cost

Rent

$9,000.00

Utilities

$1,200.00

Wages and Salaries

$9,200.00

Advertising

$4,000.00

Insurance

$340.00

Legal and Accounting

$300.00

Office Expenses

$2,500.00

Repair and Maintenance

$250.00

Telephone

$400.00

Miscellaneous Expenses

$1,000.00

Cost of Goods Sold

$2,000.00

Billing & Collection Fees

$2,900.00

TOTAL EXPENSES
$33,090.00

Wow, grossing over $40,000 per month doesn't seem like such a big deal anymore after all, now does it?

Disappointed? Don't be, because you don't need the headaches that Mr. Martial Arts Magnate has. He has to teach classes for about 20-30 hours a week, plan his marketing and advertising for about another 5 hours per week, plan and implement internal marketing promotions and special events for about another 5 hours per week, perform administrative work for about 10-12 hours per week, manage and train his employees for about another 5 hours per week, and perform miscellaneous duties for about another 5 hours per week.

That's about a 60-hour workweek, on average, plus all the headaches that 400 clients, five employees, and their families can bring. Oh, that's right; I forgot to mention the families of the students. Since most of the clients Mr. Magnate has are kids, he has to deal with their parents as well. That's like having 600 clients to service for every 200 kids you have in your school.

I can guess what you're thinking right now: working yourself into an early grave in the corporate sector doesn't seem so bad after hearing all that. But wait! I haven't explained how a "Small Dojo Big Profits" school owner does it! Aren't you the least bit curious how his or her budget and expenses look? Well, okay then, let's give some hypothetical numbers a once over and see how they compare.

The "Small Dojo Big Profits" Approach to Budgeting and Expenses

Remember earlier in the chapter when I talked about "waste not, want not?" You are about to see this philosophy in action and witness the powerful effect it can have on your school's profit margins.

Let's review what we came up with in the last chapter for the small dojo owner's gross tuition collections in his or her 1,500 square foot studio; 240 students at $99 per month base tuition = $23,760 in gross tuition collections per month. But, using the same figures we used for Mr. Magnate we'll calculate the gross tuition collections and testing fees for our small school owner to be at $26,400 per month. Notice that the tuition collected is higher because we don't follow fads and trends but instead stick with our niche market; therefore every student in our studio is paying a minimum of $99 per month tuition. Adding in Pro Shop sales and special events will easily put us in the $30,000 per month range for the gross profit in our small studio.

Now, let's look at the expenses for our small studio:

Rent – We already determined that this would be about $2,400, but if you look hard enough, you will probably be able to get a location for less.

Utilities – Figure about $250.00 per month including waste, water, and sewage.

Wages and Salaries – The small school owner only needs one other person in the school with him or her to run things, and that's the front office person. Also, she only needs that individual to work about 25 hours per week, since the owner tends the phones during the day while performing other tasks such as cleaning and bookkeeping (this is effective multi-tasking, which is one of the strategies a "Small Dojo Big Profits" studio owner uses to maximize their effort while minimizing expenses). If you can convince your spouse or significant other to assist you by working in the office your expenses in this area will be even less. As for assistant instructors, the school owner utilizes a well-developed leadership team comprised of students from within each class they teach. Cost for this labor: zero cost for assistant instructors, $1,500 per month for a front office assistant.

Advertising – The small school owner will rely heavily on effective advertising to bring in new customers; however, much of that advertisement will consist of low-cost marketing methods (discussed in detail in chapter 10). Still, he or she should commit to spending about 10% of their gross each month on advertising. Cost of advertising: $2,500 per month.

Insurance – Insurance costs are less due to having fewer students; $200 per month.

Legal and Accounting Expenses – The small school owner has less bookkeeping work and handles much of it himself; cost is $150 per month.

Office Expenses – Office expenses are also greatly reduced due to the fact that there are not as many students to service and because with only 1,500 square feet it is not necessary to hire a cleaning service to clean the studio. Having fewer students and cleaning the dojo herself every day saves our small studio owner about $4,500 per month. Cost of office expenses: $500 per month.

Repair and Maintenance – Once again, fewer students and a smaller studio mean reduced costs: $100 per month.

Telephone – Phone & internet costs will run about the same as the big schools; $300 per month.

Miscellaneous Expenses – Same story as office expenses, smaller school means less expenditures; $500 per month.

Cost of Goods Sold – Although the small school owner may not sell as much equipment, he also doesn't have to hire an extra person to run the Pro Shop. Cost is $1,200 per month.

Billing Company Collection Fees – You are really going to like this one. The small school owner does his billing in-house, plus he only allows his clients to pay by electronic transaction or by payment in full. This brings his cost for billing services from 7% of gross collections down to a fraction of one percent. Cost of billing services: $75.00 per month plus around $200 per month for membership to an independent consulting service.

Now, let's look at how this all adds up:

Expense
Monthly Cost
Rent

$2,400.00

Utilities

$250.00

Wages and Salaries

$1,500.00

Advertising

$2,500.00

Insurance

$200.00

Legal and Accounting

$150.00

Office Expenses

$500.00

Repair and Maintenance

$100.00

Telephone/Internet

$300.00

Miscellaneous Expenses

$500.00

Cost of Goods Sold

$1,200.00

Billing & Collection Fees

$275.00

TOTAL

$9,875.00

So, for about half the work and worries our small studio owner is going to see better than twice the net profit on his small studio that Mr. Martial Arts Magnate does in his big super-dojo. Quick, somebody go give Mr. Martial Arts Magnate a gun so he can shoot himself and end his misery!

Now you can see why I say that, for the most part, martial arts business owners have been duped by the consulting companies, billing companies and industry "experts" who have been telling them that bigger schools are better.

Of course, there are always going to be exceptions to every rule. There are large school owners that have managed their schools well and are achieving much higher than average profit margins. As well, there are small studio owners who are wasteful and lackadaisical in their management that couldn't turn a profit if they won the lottery. Overall, however, the old adage "Keep it small and keep it all" is highly applicable to the martial arts industry. The bigger your school gets the more work you have to do and the harder it will be to keep making large profit margins. So, do yourself a favor and hedge your bets; keep your school small and efficient and leave the headaches and tiny profit margins to the big boys.

Practical Application of Planning and Budgeting

If you start doing some research on planning and budgeting for a small business, you will soon find that much of the information written is based on planning and budgeting for large corporations. Many of the documents you will see use confusing and intimidating formats that are based on standard corporate accounting procedures. Although I think it is important that a business owner is financially literate, and that you learn to read income statements and balance sheets (most reports that accounting software packages print are based on these two accounting report formats), I don't believe that it is necessary or even practical for you to learn this before you start writing a budget for your studio. I have found that keeping things simple in a martial arts studio is almost always easier and more efficient than using complicated systems. With this in mind, I am going to show you how to write a very simple yet effective budget for your business.

You should write your budget and business plan following the simple steps I am going to lay out over the next few pages before you ever open the doors on your studio. The more time you spend in planning beforehand, the more prepared you will be for the little unexpected bumps and turns that come up in everyday business life. Once again, remember the old adage, *"Fail to plan, and plan to fail."*

First: Know How Much Money You Need To Make

The first step in writing a budget is to know how much money you *need* to make at a bare minimum in order to keep your doors open. The table I used for our examples earlier in the chapter will work just fine for organizing and laying out your projected business expenses. You may also find it helpful to create a spreadsheet in a program like Excel, so you can play around with different figures to see how your numbers turn out.

Note that, for expenses, it is always better to use figures that are slightly higher than your projections, if only as a safety cushion in case of unexpected costs. Using the tables from earlier in this chapter as a guideline, create your own table or spreadsheet to determine your projected expenses, and then write down the total below:

Total Projected Monthly Expenses:
     $_____._____

Second: Know How Much Money You Want To Keep

Your second step is to figure out how much money you want to keep as profit at the end of each month (remember, gross is the total that you bring in; net is what you take home). Think big, but be practical!

Understand that in your first year you probably are probably not going to make the amount of money you might wish to make; but still it pays to have a solid goal for how much you eventually want to earn in net profit each month. Write it down below:

Goal for Monthly Net Profits:
    $_____._____

Third: Determine How Much You Need to Gross Each Month

Now we need to figure out how much you need to bring in every month in *gross* profit to hit your goals for *net* profit. To do this, add your Projected Monthly Expenses to your Goal for Monthly Net Profits:

Total Projected Monthly Expenses:
    $_____._____ +
Goal for Monthly Net Profits:
    $_____._____ =
Required Gross Income
    $_____._____

Fourth: Determine Your Income Sources

Now we have to determine your income sources, and how much projected income you will have to make from each source to hit your numbers each month. You can choose to only account for income made through your regular tuition collections, or you can factor in other profit centers, such as testing fees and Pro Shop sales. I always preferred to do my budget off of my projected gross tuition collections because then everything I made after that was gravy.

Either way, you must calculate how many sales, students, etcetera that you must have at a certain price point to hit your projected income goals. Use the system below as a guideline to determine the income you need to make from each source to reach your income goals:

Income from Tuition:
   # of Students _____
   x Monthly Tuition $_____._____ =
   $_____.____
   Income from Testing Fees:
   # of Students Testing/Month _____
   x Fee $_____ =
   $_____.____
   Income from Pro Shop Sales:
   # of Students _____
   x Avg. Monthly Purchase $____
   = $_____.____
   Income from Special Events:
   # of Attendees at Event _____
   x Cost of Event $_____
   = $_____.____
   Total Projected Gross Income = $_____.____

As you can see, this is a pretty straightforward process that anyone can do. There is NO excuse for you to not write out a budget for your business. Now, let's look at an example of a small dojo budget so you have an idea of just how attainable a six-figure income is when running a studio the "Small Dojo Big Profits" way.

An Example of Planning and Budgeting

Okay, let's do some budgeting and planning for our hypothetical "Small Dojo Big Profits" studio by plugging some numbers into the formulae we used in our earlier examples:

Expense
Monthly Cost

Rent

$2,400.00

Utilities

$250.00

Wages and Salaries

$1,500.00

Advertising

$2,500.00

Insurance

$200.00

Legal and Accounting Expenses

$150.00

Office Expenses

$500.00

Repair and Maintenance

$100.00

Telephone/Internet

$300.00

Miscellaneous Expenses

$500.00

Cost of Goods Sold

$1,200.00

Billing Company Collection Fees

$275.00

TOTAL
$9,875.00

Let's say our owner wants to make $10,000 per month, a reasonable amount of net income for a small studio owner that is not too hard to accomplish:

Total Projected Monthly Expenses: $ 9,875.00
   Goal for Monthly Net Profits: $10,000.00
   Required Gross Income $19,875.00

Are we good so far? Okay then, now let's see where he is going to make that money:

Income From Tuition:
   # of Students 180
   x Monthly Tuition $99.00
   = $17,820.00
   Income From Testing Fees:
   # of Students Testing/Month 60
   x Fee $25.00
   = $ 1,500.00
   Income From Pro Shop Sales:
   # of Students 180
   x Avg. Monthly Purchase $8.00
   = $1,440.00
   Income From Special Events:
   # of Attendees at Event 20
   x Fee For Event $25.00
   = $500.00
   Total Projected Gross Income = $21,260.00
   Required Gross Income = $19,875.00
   Surplus/Shortage = +$ 1,385.00

So our small school owner will be doing fairly well for herself if she makes these numbers every month. I would like you to note that these numbers are very easy to reach; building a studio enrollment of

180 students is a very attainable goal if you have scouted out a good location in a community with a sufficient population that is apt to be interested in your services.

Another point I want to mention is that these numbers do not include profits made from charging customers a down payment on their courses. This is intentional, as you may decide that you want to waive your membership fee during certain times of the year or as part of a particular marketing promotion. Therefore, I do not advise that you include income from down payments in your budget.

You quite possibly will be able to charge higher tuition rates in your area if the market will bear them. Something else that I'd like to point out is that these numbers do not reflect the increased tuition that your students will be paying in their second and third years at your studio. I be speaking more about these two issues and I'll show you how to make more income from your second and third-year students in the next chapter.

That was pretty painless, right? There were no complicated equations involved, because it isn't really necessary in our business; the income and expenses are pretty straightforward so there isn't really any need to make it complicated. Yet since budgeting is a pretty straightforward process in a martial arts school, many school owners never write one out, thinking that they can just calculate and keep their budget in their head.

This is a huge mistake! You need to know where every dime and penny is going each and every month, and you need definite guidelines and limits for what you plan to spend in each area of your studio operation that you force yourself to stick with each and every month. Then, if you miss your goals you can go back and see where you messed up, and you'll know what you need to adjust to compensate for your mistake. If you don't write out a budget and keep track of your expenses, you'll never know where you're losing money or where you need to tighten your belt up each month. So, *do not procrastinate*; write out your budget right now!

Some Final Thoughts on Expenses and Budgeting

The best way to ensure that your profit margins are high and your expenses are low is to become a cheap son-of-a-gun, a real stingy hum-dinger. And that means that you will use any ethical strategy you can find to save money on your expenses. Recruit volunteers? Definitely. Buy your supplies in bulk for less? Sure thing, sign me up. Turn off unnecessary lights and keep a close eye on the thermostat? You bet!

Anything that you can do to save on your expenses should be a no-brainer; just do it and smile. The money you save will go straight into your pocket, and you can rest easy at night knowing that you are a sharp, savvy, smart-as-a-whip business person following a business strategy that will keep your doors open for the long haul.

EIGHT

PRICING YOUR SERVICES AND ENROLLING STUDENTS

Setting Your Fees

Setting your fees is a relatively painless and simple process. Yet, many new school owners agonize over this task because they don't want to drive potential customers away by "over-pricing" their services. **This is a direct result of having a scarcity mindset instead of a prosperity mindset.** People with a scarcity mindset always think that there isn't enough money, or customers, or opportunities to go around, so they are constantly worrying about this scenario or that scenario in which their whole life falls apart around them because there simply wasn't enough to go around.

You need to instead train yourself to have a *prosperity mindset*. The entrepreneur with a prosperity mindset is opportunity and prosperity focused. Because of this, they see wealth and opportunity all around them, all the time! They don't have time to engage in fruitless conjecture about challenges they might face because they are too busy taking advantage of the opportunities they have found and continue to find on a daily basis.

Another factor that may cause school owners to falter when they approach the task of setting their fees is **self-image**. All too often, martial arts instructors fail to comprehend just how valuable their knowledge and services are to their clients. This is extremely unfortunate on many levels!

For one, you as a martial arts instructor need to have a healthy and positive self-image; otherwise, how are you going to build the same in your students? Second, if you do not value your services, then I can assure you, no one else will. Third, by under-valuing your services, you are actually driving your best clients away. That's right, instead of drawing in more students by having lower rates; you will be chasing them away by the droves!

Success Strategy: *Develop a positive attitude, because the difference between success and failure is often found in a person's attitude.*

Let me explain. Social scientists, psychologists, and sales and marketing experts all agree that value is based on perception. Think for a minute about how people determine value and worth. Much of our perception of the value and worth of a product is determined by our beliefs as to how using that product or service will enhance or damage our standing within our peer group.

As I write this, I am reminded of $900 handbags, $2,000 watches, and $4,000 designer dresses, not to mention $100,000 sports cars. Although these products may arguably be of a higher quality than similar, less costly items, consumers are more than willing to pay inflated prices for them due to their perception as a symbol of status in our culture. What is even more interesting to note is that much of that perception is based on the price that the manufacturer demands for the product!

Amazingly, consumers will often go to great lengths to purchase such products. I just read an article the other day in the Wall Street Journal that described how designer handbags are all the rage in Japan right now. Secretaries and factory workers are spending their entire savings and maxing out their credit in order to fill their closets with $1,200 handbags. I know it sounds ridiculous and that this is an extreme example, but this is highly illustrative of the power of perceived value. So, if you can get the customer to appraise your services as being valuable and exclusive, they will have very little objection to your charging reasonable rates for your instruction.

There is one final point I would like to make about pricing your services. People generally know how much they are going to have to spend before going out to shop for a particularly expensive product or service. Chances are good that they looked at brochures and ads, spoke to their friends, or shopped around on the internet before they decided to go out to make that purchase. This means that they will usually know approximately how much they can expect to pay for martial arts classes when they walk through your doors.

I must tell you that in all my years of teaching classes and running schools, ***ninety percent of the objections I heard from clients that were inquiring about classes had nothing to do with price.*** Most of the objections you will hear will have to do with time and commitment. But, in those rare instances when someone did in fact object to the price, I was nearly always able to work around their objections and get them enrolled.

Even so, I am going to give you a tactic that you can use in your ads and enrollment procedures that will nearly eliminate all price objections before a potential client even comes in to your studio! With this method, your prospects will be pre-sold on your basic tuition rate from the time they cross your doorstep. But before I get to that, let's talk a little bit about martial arts tuition, setting your fees, and inflation.

Why the Martial Arts Industry is Twenty Years Behind the Economy

In 1965, commercial martial arts studios were charging $40.00 per month for tuition. In 2012 dollars, calculating for inflation, **that would be the equivalent of charging $287.30 a month for tuition.** Yet most studios today only charge in the range of $75 to $150 per month for their basic program of instruction. That puts the martial arts industry's tuition rates at nearly twenty years behind the rest of the economy! This, my dear fellow martial artists, is a travesty of immense proportions. Martial artists are cheating themselves out of their livelihood, and most of them don't even realize it.

But how did this happen? In other sectors of business, it is quite common for an industry to evaluate and adjust their prices according to the economy's rate of inflation every one to two years, so why doesn't the martial arts industry do the same? Well, I'll tell you how and why; because the "mainstream" martial arts business community is rife with incestuous business practices. Until recently, hardly anyone from the martial arts business community ever went outside of our sector to see what is going on in other areas of enterprise, and they rarely kept up with the sweeping trends in business that were going on all around them. Accordingly, the same old ideas and concepts keep getting passed around among us, and it has been rare that anyone ever brought in any new and current business ideas into our industry. So, the economy just passed us by.

Now, the reason behind this is simple; for the most part, martial artists are trained from day one to "toe the line" and follow the leader. We are taught that it is not okay to do something differently from the way we were taught to do it, nor is it okay to improve upon or add to what our teachers taught us. Those who innovate are the subject of much controversy and debate in the martial arts world; this in turn discourages a great number of people from becoming innovators in the practice of their art. Knowing this, then why should it be any different for us when it comes to our martial arts businesses?

What this Means to You

It is extremely important for your future success that you take note of this inconsistency between our industry and the mainstream of American business. It can be argued that our industry's hesitation to increase our rates is stunting our growth as a whole.

Nevertheless, you as a school owner owe it to yourself to charge a reasonable rate for your services. It doesn't take a math genius to figure out that it is a whole lot easier and more profitable to run a school that has 180 students paying $149 a month tuition each than it is to run a school with 300 students paying $69 each per month. Given the choice, which will you choose; struggling to get by charging 1970's era rates, or happily making a tidy profit every month charging rates that are in tune with the current economy and increases in the cost of living?

How to Determine Your Rates

To determine your tuition rates, you first have to answer a few questions:

1. **Do you have any competition in your area?** If you are the only school, you can pretty much set the rates for your area, within the limits of what the market will bear. Obviously, if you are going to open in a middle-class area, you can't expect your clients to pay $250 per month per person. However, if you were opening a school in West Palm Beach, you might consider charging such rates.

2. **What is the bare minimum you will charge for tuition?** I am going to spell this out for you; you should be charging no less than $99.00 per month for group classes. If you take into account the calculations we made for inflation, $99 per month is roughly equal to 1983

rates. How the heck do you think you are going to be able to pay your bills if you are charging any less than that? In my opinion, anyone that is charging less than $100 per month for their classes may as well be teaching for free.

3. **What are the going rates in your area among the existing competitors?** When you do your research on this, don't count part-time programs like those at the YMCA. These guys are not your competition; don't even give them a thought. For pricing purposes the businesses that you SHOULD be looking at as your competition for kids programs are **dance studios, gymnastics centers, and cheerleading camps**. For adults I would suggest checking out **golf instruction, dance lessons, flying lessons, and continuing education classes.** Have you checked the prices on these activities lately? You should, because they are way ahead of us in pricing their services. When I started teaching full-time in the mid-nineties, I was shocked that some of my clients were paying three times as much to put their kids in gymnastics lessons as I was charging for my classes, and these were working-class folks! Check out the competition, and if they are charging **more** than $100 per month for two group sessions a week, you should charge about 10% less for your services, but charge no less than $99 per month. If they are charging **less** than $99 per month, you should still charge $99 per month at the very least.

Some of you may be concerned that if your rates are higher than your competitors, no one will enroll in your classes. Nothing could be further from the truth. People don't mind paying a premium price for a premium service. When we get to Chapter 10 on marketing, I will show you how to position your business in your market so that you are known as the premium service among your target clientele. Trust me; once you do this, people will line up to pay your prices.

Important Point: *If people regard your services as having an innate value, they will be more than willing to pay a premium for access to those services.*

Setting Price and Payment Plans

I have seen all kinds of methods of setting membership payment plans. I have seen courses where you pay by the belt, by the number of techniques you learn, by the hours of instruction; it goes on and on and on. However, in my experience the best way to break down your membership payment plans is in a way that is easy for you to explain and easy for the client to understand. If you make it too complicated, it will make your job harder during enrollment conferences because the client will think that you are trying to confuse them; this makes them suspicious and they will be harder to close (closing should be easy, by the way, if you do things right from the beginning; more on that later in this chapter). You MUST be an advocate for your client if you want to succeed in business, so make it easy for them and you will make things easier on you.

The simplest method of breaking down your membership payment plans is by the year and month. Your minimum length of membership should be 12 months (don't worry, I am going to show you how to overcome the time commitment objection) so you should have your rates listed by the year and month on your rate sheet when you conduct an enrollment "conference." In the MartialArtSchoolAlliance.com website document archive I provide a sample "Programs and Payment Options" sheet that you can use in your own studio or you can type up your own. Just be sure to break down your rate plan by the yearly rate, then by the initial payment and the monthly payment, and include information on family discounts and discounts for pre-payment (sometimes called "cash outs"). Make this document easy to read, since you are going to be displaying it to your prospects when you enroll them in your programs.

A Word of Caution: If you use the term "finance" in your presentation or materials, you must follow all truth in lending laws for your state and area. Check with your attorney regarding this issue. The last thing you want is the state attorney general breathing down your neck just because of an honest oversight regarding a technicality of the law.

Getting back to pricing, when typing up your rates, always use "7's" and "9's" at the end of all your prices (this is known as "even-odd" pricing in marketing-speak). For instance, instead of $130 per month use a rate of $129 per month; instead of $100 per month use a rate of $97 or $99 per month, and so on. Marketing and sales experts figured out a long time ago that when a person sees a price like $29, psychologically they perceive the price to be $20 instead of $30; even though they know that it is closer to $30.

It may seem like an insignificant adjustment, but it will make a big difference in how your clients evaluate the expense of your rates. Just remember that you should never use "5's" at the end of your rates or round up your prices to the nearest ten; it doesn't work. Don't ask me why, but ending prices in "7's" and "9's" has been proven to be advantageous, so I recommend that you stick with that method.

Membership Fees and "Down Payments"

Generally, you will want to charge a yearly membership fee for each student when they enroll or renew, to help defray the costs of wear and tear on your equipment and facility. $100 per year is sufficient; if you multiply that number by 250 students it is the equivalent of $25,000 per year in additional revenues that you would not collect otherwise. For $25,000 a year, you should be able to keep your studio and equipment looking pretty nice. You will collect this fee along with the new student's first month's tuition when they enroll, and on their anniversary date when they renew. I recommend that you set this money aside in an interest-bearing account so it is available for its intended purpose when needed; at the end of the year, any unused portion can be paid to you as a distribution from your company.

By the way, I hate the term "down payment," because like it or not, it has an ugly connotation due to its abuse in our own and in other industries. I prefer to use the term "initial payment," as it is a more accurate term for the client's first payment. You can call it what you like, but I have found that making small changes in my language when discussing money with clients makes a world of difference in their attitude toward the transaction.

Success Strategy: *Use the proper language to put clients at ease.*

Tuition Payments

While some schools like to encourage their clients to pay up front for their memberships, I have never really pushed "cash outs." Instead, I have always preferred to have a steady monthly income of payments coming in to my bank account each month. Cash has a tendency to get spent, and I have witnessed more than one martial arts instructor who did a good deal of their business using them that ended up regretting it when they found that their classes were full but their monthly cash flow and bank account had dwindled down to next to nothing. Still, it doesn't hurt to take cash up front every now and then, so long as you save it in your interest bearing account along with your membership fees.

You will usually accept the client's initial payment by cash, check, or credit card at your studio when they enroll; all subsequent monthly payments are then made electronically to you directly. I like to break it down into one initial payment when they enroll and 11 equal monthly payments for the year thereafter. I advise avoiding the practice of "shorting" their payments by setting up larger monthly payments over fewer months. Since most of your students will enroll during three key periods of the year: early fall, January, and early summer; shorting their payments can create fluctuations in your monthly tuition collections, which in turn makes budgeting more difficult.

Also, don't ever allow someone to pay quarterly at the school; it is too difficult to track, and eventually you'll have a ton of people wanting to do it. Just tell them that once they are set up with the billing company, they can pay their tuition anyway they like, so long as it is paid on time. Generally, these people just want to avoid making a long-term commitment; stick to your policies and don't fall for it when they request this type of billing arrangement.

Enrolling Students

Three words: easy as pie, *if* you are honest with your prospective clients and you believe in the value of your services. Enrolling a new student should be the simplest and most enjoyable aspect of your business, outside of promoting your students to black belt. In my opinion, too many people in this industry make too big of a deal about closing the sale, when the fact is, **any person that walks in your door already wants to buy what you have.** Over-complicating the process of making a sale to a person that already wants what you have is just plain dumb. Oh wait, did I say that? Well, it is dumb, what else can I say?

Three Universal Rules for Selling Anything

Three universal rules hold true no matter what you are selling; cars, boats, houses, jewelry, long distance service, or martial arts school memberships. The three rules are pretty simple concepts, yet they represent the collective wisdom of many thousands of successful salespeople. Keep them in mind at all times when dealing with potential clients and you will see a sharp increase in your numbers. The three rules are:

1. **Rule #1: Everyone likes to buy, but no one likes the idea of being sold.** People simply do not like "hard-sell" tactics. Even if you get them to buy using a hard sell approach, they are going to be pretty raw about being talked into making their purchase and you will have problems with them later on down the road. Stick to the "soft-sell" to build good customer relations from the start.

2. **Buying is an emotional, not a rational, process.** No matter the intellect or disposition of the individual, on some level they are buying your product to fulfill some emotional need they have. *If you can get them to believe that your product will make them smarter, safer, wealthier, or better looking (and you can back those claims up) they will buy from you.* As a rule of thumb, always try to discover what the client's emotional need or motivation is before you make your sales presentation.

3. **After the sale is made, the buyer must be able to rationalize their purchase to remain satisfied with their decision.** In marketing-speak, the phenomenon that occurs when a consumer purchases a product and later develops regrets about purchasing

that product is called **dissonance** (sometimes this is called buyer's remorse). Dissonance is bad. To avoid dissonance, give your client plenty of facts and information about why you are a great instructor and why your school is the best place to train so they can easily rationalize their decision to train at your school, and make sure that you can back up all those claims.

Although most of us are intuitively aware of these concepts, few if any salespeople ever give any thought to applying them in their approach. Using them will give you a "psychological edge" over your competition and keep you one step ahead of the game when presenting your programs to a prospective client. However, failing to use them can have dire consequences; so ignore them at your own peril.

Pre-Selling and Posture: The Keys to Easy Enrollments

To ensure a higher closing rate, I prefer the techniques of "pre-selling" and "posture" to any other sales method. "Pre-selling" is just what it says; selling your prospect on your product before the sale is actually made. "Posture" is nurturing an internal attitude that says "I have the deal" and "The buyer wants what I have." This immediately puts you in a position of control with your prospects. Please note that having posture does not mean acting in an arrogant manner; instead, consider it as the opposite of being "desperate" to make a sale.

Using pre-selling and having posture in your presentation are highly effective methods of ensuring that you quickly and easily close every single person that walks through your door. But, how exactly do you pre-sell a prospect on joining as a regular member? Well, we are going to take a three-step approach to pre-selling a prospect on our services.

Those 3 Steps to Pre-selling Are:

1. **First, Pre-sell in the ad that gets them to call or come in.** We are going to give them an offer they can't refuse by promising to give them a solution to their need at a price they can afford. We will do this by using **psychological triggers to elicit a strong emotional response** in our prospect. This in turn will encourage the prospect to act immediately in contacting us, instead of procrastinating and forgetting to call. We'll go over this in more detail when we discuss marketing, but for right now, just understand that using the proper language in your ad is the first step to pre-selling your prospects.

2. **Second, pre-sell them over the phone or when they walk in the door.** The way we are going to do that is to *listen, listen, listen* to what they have to tell us. We are going to treat them like they are the most important person in the world at that moment, because they are. We will ask the right questions in order to glean from them just exactly what their need or problem is, listen intently to the answers, then we are going to again give them an offer they can't refuse by giving them a solution that meets the needs they just described to us at a price they can afford. This is what is known as the "consultant mindset" in selling; you position yourself as an advocate for the consumer, not as their adversary. To do this you must gain their trust, and from that point on, do nothing to violate that trust and everything you can to encourage it.

3. **Third, pre-sell them during your Introductory Course.** The way we do this is to show them, not tell

them, but **show them** what our classes can do to meet the needs they expressed to us when we first spoke with them. We are going to **prove that we have the solution to their problem**, so that when it comes time to enroll them on a regular program, they are pre-sold on becoming a regular member.

Okay, so you're saying, "Well, that sounds easy enough, but how do I actually go about enrolling them?" We'll cover effective advertising in the next chapter, so for now let's start with the telephone....

The Lifeline of Your Studio

The office telephone is the most important piece of equipment you will have in your studio. Without it, your business will never grow or prosper in the manner or to the extent you desire. Answering the telephone incorrectly can cause you to lose more potential customers than most any other mistake you can make in your business. Therefore, you need to make certain that you understand good telephone protocol and that you hone your phone skills to a fine art; that way you will rarely if ever let a prospect slip through your fingers due to mishandling their phone call.

Handling Phone Inquiries

Most every telephone inquiry can be handled in a few simple steps.

First, be sure to answer the phone in a professional manner. Studies have shown that the average person forms an opinion about someone within the first 5 seconds of their initial contact; therefore it is extremely important that everyone who answers the phone at your studio be as professional and courteous as possible. To this end, every staff member should be familiar with the following guidelines for properly answering the phone:

- Always identify yourself to the caller. They may not remember your name, but it is just good protocol. "ABC Karate, this is Mr. Massie speaking, how may I help you?"
- Always sound professional and courteous.
- Your manner of speech should be grammatically correct.
- When speaking with clients, you should keep your religious and political beliefs to yourself.
- Always sound glad that the person on the line called.
- Smile! It will make your voice sound warmer and friendlier. If you have a difficult time with this, keep a mirror on your desk and watch yourself when you are on the phone.

Next, always get a name and phone number from the caller. Without getting this contact information, you'll have no way of contacting the prospect if you need to at a later date.

Third, find out who they're calling for, and the age of the prospect. This is vital information! You must know the age of the prospective student to properly address their needs.

Fourth, find out the caller's motivation/need/desire, their reason for calling. This is the key piece of information you need to pre-sell your program. You want to ask them what benefits they wish to receive through taking martial arts classes, then...

Fifth, inform them of how your programs can answer their needs. If you listened carefully and asked the right questions earlier in the call, this should be a piece of cake. DON'T LIE! If the caller wants tai chi, and you teach BJJ, don't tell them you teach "something similar." I know it sounds like I am beating a dead horse on this honesty issue, but it is important that you understand there are much better ways to get customers than by lying to them. Remember the consultant mindset!

Sixth, schedule the introductory lesson. Once you

inform them of how you can meet their needs, simply say, "Great, I have an appointment for an Introductory Lesson at ___:oo on _____, or at ___:oo on _____; which time would work better for you?" Always give them two choices; nine times out of ten they'll pick the first one, but for some reason giving the caller two choices elicits a higher conversion rate.

Seventh, handle price inquiries. This can get a little sticky, so pay attention. The average caller has no idea what to ask you, so the first thing out of their mouth is "How much is it?" Stick to the sample script that follows and you will head off any objections regarding price AND pre-qualify your prospect for the sale.

Eighth, verify information. Obviously, it's not going to do you a darn bit of good to write down the caller's contact information if it's wrong. Be sure to verify their phone number and appointment time before you end the call. Also, make certain that the caller knows where your studio is located.

Ninth, document the information and appointment. Keep records of everything! I have some log sheets on the MartialArt-SchoolAlliance.com website that you can copy and use for this purpose.

Finally, notify the instructor who is responsible for teaching the Introductory Lesson that the appointment has been set. Communication is extremely important; I keep a whiteboard calendar on the office wall on which I post all the appointments for the next 14 days. That way, everyone on staff is aware of what's coming down the pipe.

The most important thing to remember about handling information calls is that your only purpose when speaking to a potential client is to set an appointment for an introductory lesson. Failing that, it is to get their contact information so you can follow up with them at a later date. Accordingly, your conversation should be "to the point" and you should stick to the script outline. Remember, "The more you tell, the less you sell."

Sample Phone Script

(*Phone rings – smile when you pick up the phone – it makes your voice sound much more warm and friendly*)

ABC Karate Academy, this is Mr. Massie speaking. Thank you for calling. How may I help you? And who am I speaking with? (*write it down*) *Are you calling for yourself or for someone else? What's (his/her) name (write it down) How old is he/she?* (*write it down*) *How did you hear about us?* (*write it down*) *What benefits are you hoping that a martial arts program will bring to (name)? (or) What motivated you to call us today?* (*Whatever they say, write it down*)

We have a lot of (parents/students) that have enrolled at ABC Karate for just that reason. The best thing for you to do would be to stop in and let us show you our programs and give you a copy of our schedule. We have a (state your current intro special) that includes (state what they get) for just (state your special discount price). Would you be able to stop in this afternoon? (*if not, schedule an alternate time and be sure to write it down in your calendar*)

Great! Can I get your number in case something comes up and we have to reschedule? (*write it down*) *Do you have an email address? I'd be glad to send you a copy of our newsletter – it would give you more of a feel for our studio.* (*write it down*)*Do you know where we're located?* (*Tell them anyway*) *So, we'll see you (day) at (time). Be sure to call us if you have to reschedule, because our appointments fill up quickly and we wouldn't want to make you wait to get started. Thanks for calling.*

(*If they do not set an appointment for an intro course*)

If you'll give me your address I'll send you some

information that you can look over to give you some background on our studio. (write it down and send that info out as soon as you get off the phone)

Morality and Ethics: Essentials for Success in Selling

As you may have already determined, this is a subject that I have very strong feelings about, and I would like to share a few thoughts on having integrity in your sales approach. I've already stated more than once in this manual that dishonest practices hurt our industry. I want you to know that you don't have to use dishonest business practices to be successful; honesty and good common sense in dealing with people will carry you further than any dishonest method of turning a quick buck ever will.

Now, as far as enrolling new students goes, the question always comes up: "Should I take cash up front or should I enroll everyone on a monthly payment plan?" I know that this has become a big issue in the industry, and I am going to tell you the truth; cash outs are better than monthly payments, but only under the following conditions:

1. You can manage your money and are disciplined in your spending habits. It won't do you a bit of good to make $50,000 in cash outs in one month if you spend it the next.

2. You are diligently working on constantly improving the value of the service you offer your clients. That doesn't necessarily mean that you have to kill yourself to do this; just make sure that you are teaching the best classes you possibly can, and that you do lots of the little things that don't take a lot of effort to do but that your students really appreciate (like knowing everyone's name, sending them cards on their birthday, and so forth).

If you adhere to the above conditions, yes, cash outs are great, despite my personal preference for monthly payments. Speaking purely from a profit perspective, I'd much rather get $3,700 up front for a two year membership than to be getting monthly payments for the first year and have the student quit the second and end up not paying for the rest of the membership.

There is nothing wrong with using cash outs when you are offering a really, really great service to your clients, you are working hard to keep them happy, and you are constantly motivating them to take full advantage of their pre-paid memberships. But, if your classes are horrible and your customer service sucks, then doing cash outs is wrong. Let's face it, it's just plain dishonest to take someone's money, knowing full-well that they are not going to get their money's worth from your service.

If you aren't 100% confident in your program quality or customer service, you should work on that aspect of your business before you start trying to find ways to increase your profits. Take it from me - chances are good that if your programs are awesome, the money will follow just the same, regardless of how you collect your tuition.

Providing Full Disclosure

On a related note, be sure to tell the client up front about all the costs of attending your program and what they are for. Being up front and honest when enrolling a new student will increase your credibility with that client. There are also a few things you'll want to avoid in your disclosure of fees and costs:

- Don't tell them that your down payment is for an "administrative fee." Even if it's the truth, too many businesses have used this as a lame excuse to overcharge their clients, and you'll get some backlash on it.
- Don't make up reasons for charging a membership fee or down payment, like for instance telling them that they

have to have insurance coverage to attend your school and that's what the down payment is for (especially when you know darn good and well that your insurance only covers you and not your students).

- Don't try to hide the fact that you charge testing or other additional fees.
- And for goodness sakes, don't obscure the fact that they are signing a binding contract when they sign your Membership Agreement!

If you do attempt to obscure the truth when you enroll new members, you will lose credibility with them and possibly lose a future client. Besides, eventually, they will find out the truth about your fees anyway. Even if you do fool them at the outset, expect to hear about it from them later and to pay in spades for being dishonest with them. Also, you could be held criminally and civilly liable for your actions in a court of law. I think we all will agree that making a few thousand dollars is not worth risking jail time over...

By the way, I am not making this stuff up; these are all actual sales tactics and procedures that various billing companies have told their clients to use in the past. I have personally attended seminars and trainings where the staff of large billing and consultation companies basically told the participants to lie to their clients in order to close a sale. Also, I have acquaintances who continue to do business with these companies, and they keep me informed as to the latest schemes and tricks they are coming up with for their member studios.

I warn you, once you get involved in the industry you are going to be exposed to these types of tactics as well. My advice to you when someone tells you to use an unethical business tactic is to just nod your head until they're gone, and then forget that you had that conversation with them.

Success Strategy: *Although you may have been told that honesty is its own reward, I am here to tell you: honesty pays.*

Okay, moving on... it's time to talk about Overcoming Objections!

Overcoming Objections Using a Guarantee

Overcoming objections is a simple process that has been over-complicated by our industry. I can tell you from my own experience, building rapport with the client through using the consultant mindset approach is the best way to overcome objections before they come up. Look at it this way; if you've already been honest and forthright about your rates, price should never be an issue. If you've shown your prospective client how you can assist them with their needs, program quality should never be a problem. If you have acted as an advocate for the client, and set your schedule with flexibility and the client's convenience in mind, time conflicts should never come up. I could go on and on, but I'm sure you get the point.

However, there will be occasions when you won't be able to head off every objection before the time comes to enroll the client. In those situations, you are going to have to be able to deal with the objection effectively and in such a manner that you retain the client's trust. Many of the manuals I have read address this subject by providing a script that you are supposed to follow by rote when handling each individual objection, an approach that is guaranteed to make you sound stilted and forced in your interaction with the prospective member.

Because of this, I developed a slightly different approach to handling objections and enrolling students. You see, I am a big proponent of the old adage, "Give a man a fish, feed him for a day; teach a man to fish, feed him for life." In other words, experience has proven to me that it is far better to understand the principles and concepts behind a particular sales technique; this allows you to use it to effectively deal with any situation that may arise.

This realization has had a positive effect on both my martial arts training and my business approach. In keeping with this philosophy, I came up with a step-by-step method of dealing with any objection regardless of what it is so I wouldn't have to memorize a script. It turned out to be a very effective method and it has worked for everyone we have trained to use it.

The Five Simple Steps to Overcoming Any Objection:

1. **Root out the real objection.** There is no way to deal with the issue at hand unless you understand what exactly it is. While the client may say something to the effect of "I need to think about it" they haven't really given you the real reason for their hesitation. Asking them to specifically identify what is holding them back will allow you to focus your efforts on the real issues.

2. **Acknowledge the client's perspective.** You should do this by repeating their objection back to them, followed by an acknowledgment that you can appreciate their perspective.

3. **Address the real issue directly and honestly.** Address their concerns by honestly informing them just how your programs address those specific concerns. Be honest; lying will only get you in hot water, and it shouldn't be necessary. Remember, the consultant mindset in selling requires that you provide a real solution to the client's needs.

4. **Offer them a Thirty-Day guarantee.** For some studio owners, guarantees are an anathema. They think, "Well what if they actually take advantage of the guarantee?" In my opinion, however, if you are truly

offering a great service and outstanding value, rarely if ever will anyone take you up on your offer. Even if someone does, all that a basic thirty-day guarantee says is they have thirty days to evaluate your services with no obligation. If they leave, you haven't lost anything, and you have rid yourself of a potential headache. This is a "win-win" situation, all the way around.

5. **Ask an open-ended question to get a confirmation of the client's willingness to seal the deal.** You have to get an indication that you have dealt with the client's objection before going to the close, but you don't want to allow the prospect to say "no." An open-ended question does not require a "yes or no" answer and therefore keeps the dialogue open. However, there are exceptions to this rule. For example, if you ask the prospect, "How does that sound?" and they say, "I still don't know if I am ready to join" you need to go back to step #1 until you root out the real objection using closed-ended questions. "Is it the schedule?" "Is it the instructor?" "Is it the time commitment?" "Then, and be honest with me, it's okay; is it the cost?" Once you figure out the real objection, deal with it using steps two through four and then ask another open-ended question to get an indication that they are ready to buy. Once they tell you something to the effect of "That sounds good" or "I like that" a few times, then they are ready to enroll.

Using this five-step approach allowed us to have a 95% closing rate on students that completed our introductory course. You should memorize these five simple steps so you can easily flow with any situation and handle any objection.

Examples of Overcoming Objections

In order for you to see this methodology in action, let's examine some specific examples of how you might handle common objections. Once you see this method in action through examining a few common scenarios, I believe you'll see how easy it is to overcome any objection using the simple system I described above.

Sample Objection #1:

"My child is very aggressive; I'm afraid she'll hurt someone with what she learns here."

Now, if you have presented the proper image in your advertisement and marketing materials, this objection really should not come up. If it does, here's how you should respond. I have typed areas of specific importance in bold letters:

Response:

"Mrs. Smith, let me make sure I understand you correctly. You are concerned that your daughter will use what she learns here for the wrong reason? (Insert client response) I can see how you might think that, what with all the violence in the movies and on TV today. However, here at ABC Karate, we teach our students that martial art training is for self-improvement, not fighting.

We spend a great deal of time teaching non-violent conflict resolution skills, so your child will in fact learn to be a more peaceful person through participating in our programs. *Although I* *want your daughter to enjoy the benefits that our program will provide him, the last thing we want is for you to be dissatisfied.*

So, what I will do is give you a 30-day-guarantee. If, at any time within the first thirty days of your membership you are not completely satisfied, you may leave with no further obligation. How does that sound?"

Notice how in the response you are not even addressing the issue of "self-defense." You only want to emphasize the peaceful side of your program; with this particular objection, you absolutely do not want to encourage the idea that the child will be involved in violent aggression at all.

Unless the client has expressed that they want their child to learn self-defense skills, you would not use the term "self-defense" in your response. This is an important point; in selling, you should always use language that mirrors that of the client.

Sample Objection # 2:

"I am afraid I will get injured."

This is a common objection in schools that run hardcore martial arts programs. It usually comes up because the client has been improperly introduced to the training at the school; maybe they watched an advanced class in action or their first introduction to training was watching a sparring class. This is why it is important to set appointments when people call your studio; you get to control what the first impression of your school is.

Your job in overcoming this type of objection is to find out specifically what they are afraid of. Then, you should ensure the prospective client that they will start off in a group of complete beginners, that they will not start sparring right away, that contact is voluntary, and so on:

Response:

"Ms. Smith, what aspect of what you have seen here at ABC Karate are you concerned with? (Insert client response) While I understand your apprehension, I can assure you that this is not the case. Our mission is to offer a safe, friendly environment in which people like yourself can experience the benefits of participating in a properly instructed martial arts program.

Here at ABC Karate, your safety is our first concern. I really want you to benefit from our program, but the last thing we want is to have a student in our program that isn't enjoying their classes.

So, what I will do is give you a 30-day-guarantee on your membership. If, at any time within the first thirty days of your membership you are not completely satisfied, you may discontinue your training with no further obligation. How does that sound to you?"

Notice that the in the response the school representative is sensitive to the client's concerns, and acknowledges their feelings. It is extremely important that you do not dismiss the fears a prospective client has out of hand. The simple act of acknowledging their fear let's them know that you value their perspective and serves to strengthen the rapport you have with them.

Sample objection #3:

"I'm not sure that we want to commit to a twelve month membership."

In this case, it is important that you are up front with the client, yet that you offer a guarantee to ease their fears. The first thing you need to do is to remind them of the benefits they want to achieve through participation in your program, and then point out that those benefits are not going to be realized overnight. The way you word this response is very important, so pay close attention:

Response:

"Mrs. Jones, what you are saying is that you aren't sure that your son will stay committed to our program for a full year, is that correct? (Insert client response) That's a valid concern, and one that I commonly hear from parents who desire to enroll their children in our studio. You expressed earlier that you desire improved self-confidence and self-esteem for your son. I have to tell you that although we have a very effective program for assisting children in improving their confidence, it takes time for us to do so.

Martial art training is a very time-intensive activity; the skills and benefits that are gained from the martial arts take time to develop. That is why we only offer our services to those who are committed to putting in the time and effort to realize those benefits. Although I want your son to enjoy the benefits that our program will provide him, the last thing we want is to have a student in our program who doesn't want to be here.

So, what I will do is give you a 30-day-right-to-cancel on your membership. If, at any time within the first thirty days of your membership you are not completely satisfied, you may cancel your membership with no further obligation.

However, if your son enjoys our program and you are satisfied with the service you are

receiving, then you agree to stay for the entire year. How do you feel about that?"

As you can see, this is a very simple approach to dealing with objections and enrolling new students. Although you should have a good idea of how your studio addresses common issues that clients have about training, with this method, it is not necessary to memorize a specific script for closing a sale. So long as you use the five steps, you will be able to deal with most any objection.

One last thing I would like to mention is that it is not necessary to overcome every objection. This is where having posture in your sales presentation is very important. If you are dealing with a client that has an issue that you have not been able to address to their satisfaction, just politely say to them, "Well, we understand that not every student is right for our school. That's why we use an introductory program to interview each prospective student to see if they will be a good fit for our program."

You have merely informed the prospect that your program is exclusive and that not everyone who applies gets accepted. However, what you have accomplished by making this simple statement is to use the concept of posture to turn the tables on the prospective member. This simple approach taps into a pair of powerful psychological phenomena that are found in virtually every human being; the need to be accepted and the tendency to seek the approval of others.

In my school, we definitely did not accept just anyone into our programs; if I thought a student was not ready for training, or that their parents would be disruptive to our operations, I would politely tell them that they were not right for our program, and direct them to another studio. Because our business plan did not require a large enrollment, we were able to be more selective in who we chose to train.

That's the beauty of the "Small Dojo Big Profits" system; you don't have to have a zillion students to stay in profit, so you are never desperate to enroll a client. This takes tons of pressure off of you in your enrollment conferences, and places you firmly in the driver's seat with your clients, versus their having the power of veto over your presentation. In my opinion, that's the only way to go!

Success Strategy: *Avoid giving the impression that anyone can be accepted into your programs. Create an air of exclusivity when describing your programs to put yourself in a position of control with the prospect.*

Using the Correct Language in Your Sales Presentations

As I stated before, making slight adjustments in your language when dealing with clients can make quite a difference in your closing rate. Certain words and phrases illicit a negative response from prospective clients, and they should be avoided in your conversations. Here are a few suggestions for using the correct language when speaking with your clients:

- Instead of saying "contract," say "membership agreement."
- Instead of "price" or "cost," use the term "investment."
- Do not speak of "signing up" a new student or "closing a sale;" instead, refer to it as "joining the studio" or "enrolling in a program."
- Don't speak of "problems;" instead, use the term "challenge."

More on Posture

Your posture can make or break the sale when making a presentation about the services and programs that your studio offers. You must be confident and poised when talking about your programs and the benefits they provide, as well as when you are discussing price and length of commitment. If you falter or doubt yourself when presenting a program to a prospective client, they will pick up on your lack of confidence and wonder what you are trying to hide.

There are certain things you can do to keep your confidence high and to retain your posture when dealing with clients:

- **First, you must believe in the value of your programs.** Pull out a sheet of paper or start a new text document on your computer and write "Our programs are the best around because:" at the top of the page. Then, below the title of the page write out a list of all the benefits that can be gained from participation in your programs and number them accordingly. Post this list up by your desk and read it aloud 10 times a day, every day when you get to the office.

- **Second, you must care about the person and not the sale.** I know this sounds like some kind of "doing not-doing" Zen thing, but hear me out. If you are only intent on making the sale, and have no interest in helping the client achieve their goals, not only will they pick up on it but you need to ask yourself if you are in the right line of work. Martial arts instructors need to enjoy helping people, because helping others is at the core of what we do. If you are the type of person who cares for others, you will quickly gain rapport and trust in the people who you present your programs to. Learn to care about the people who are coming to you for your expertise and you will make things much easier on yourself (which brings me to my next point).

- **Always, always, always – remember that you are the expert, and this person is coming to you for your expertise.** They want what you have;

otherwise, they wouldn't be asking you about your services. Always remember, when someone walks through your door, they already want to join! How can you know this for certain? Why do you think they walked in your studio in the first place? Always keep in mind that *you have the deal.*

- **Once you get the indication that someone wants to join, you don't need to go into a big long spiel about your programs. The thing to do at this point is to shut up, just hand them a pen and a membership form and take their money.** You have to know when to stop talking and take the money. Once you get a signal that the person wants to join, stop chattering and get them enrolled! If you keep trying to sell a person that is already sold, they'll start questioning why you are still trying to convince them, and you will lose them. So shut up and sell!

Okay, that just about covers pricing your services and enrolling students. My final advice to you regarding pricing and selling is to stop thinking about it and just do it. If you have any more questions on this topic, check out the suggested reading selections at the end of this book.

NINE

HOW TO GET YOUR MONEY WITHOUT GIVING IT AWAY

Don't Be a Sucker

This is one area that gets a lot of school owners. They see the big slick full-page ads in the big magazines and think, "Wow, I have to hire a martial arts billing and consultation company if I want to succeed."

All I can say to that is, well, you're a sucker if you fall for that line._As I said in the beginning of the book, the martial arts billing companies are only interested in one thing, and that's getting a cut of your money. They don't care about your students, your family, whether or not you make your mortgage and car payment, how high your rent is, or what your profit margins are. Fact is they could give a rat's behind about all those things. The only thing they are concerned with is charging you a ton of money to collect your tuition – *from seven to ten times more than what similar businesses in other industries charge for the same service!*

As you already know, I fell for their song and dance too. I tried all the major billing methods that came down the pipe; billing with consultation, pre-authorized checks, EFT only, and so on. Some companies were good, and some were awful. One company that I hired to handle the billing for my first full-time location made me wait forty-five days after they first collected my money before they paid me! As you can imagine, that put a serious crimp in my operations.

But that's not the end of the difficulties I experienced with these types of companies. Another company just offered plain bad advice, some of which I have detailed elsewhere in this manual; yet another had great consultation and customer service but lousy rates. Others were inexpensive, but had serious problems with customer service. Some sent out dated marketing materials that failed to attract clients. Overall, I have to say that my experiences with traditional martial arts tuition billing companies left a sour taste in my mouth.

However, the last major billing and consultation company I used was the worst (in fact, my experience with them was the catalyst for this book). At first, we really bought into their line. They seemed to have a lot of successful schools using their services and systems, so of course we assumed that this billing company had something to do with the success of those schools and that we might emulate their success by using the company's services.

This was a big mistake. In the time we were with them, we experienced increased complaints from our customers (one of their collection reps actually cussed out one of our clients over the phone), numerous mistakes in their billing processing (which cost us more than a few clients), and rude treatment from their staff and ownership; and for this we paid them about 7-8% of our monthly gross tuition collections every single month.

As far as their consultation services were concerned, they put very little effort into preparing their materials and events. The materials were often outdated and difficult to follow; in fact, we would get packages that were so old, they had been typed on a typewriter. Instead of updating their materials, they had been recycling the same old stuff, probably since the late '80's! When we attended events, it was just as disappointing. Since the company was too cheap to rent a facility for regional events, they were usually hosted at a member studio. This often resulted in the training schedule being changed at the last minute to accommodate the studio owner's regular classes.

Their national convention left something to be desired as well. We had our staff split up each day that we attended so we could cover all the classes and compare notes on the way home. When we got together after the convention, we discovered that on many of the subjects that were covered in the classes we attended, the presenters were giving conflicting advice – there was virtually no unified system or set method of management being taught at all!

The final straw came after the events of 9/11 and the ensuing economic crash. Many school owners were affected by these events as they occurred during a time of the year when most schools enroll a great number of students in their programs. We were no exception, and got hit hard as well. To make a long story short, at a time when we had experienced a sharp decrease in our monthly collections the billing company made a mistake in our charges; that "mistake" nearly cost us our business. After that, I couldn't take anymore, so I cancelled our contract with the company.

All-in-all, the only positive thing I can say about that company is that while we were with them we met a lot of nice, caring, committed school owners who offered us a great deal of good advice. Outside of the networking opportunities and contacts, there really isn't much else I can say about them that's at all positive. It's too bad, but it's the truth.

Soon after the last fiasco with that company, I knew there had to be a better billing method out there and I was determined to find it. A different billing company had approached me a few years back that mainly handled health club accounts; I decided to call them up and give them a try. They exceeded all my expectations by offering flexibility in our billing methods, prompt remittance of funds collected on our behalf, excellent and professional customer service on the client side as well as for owners, online access to our billing data, and the lowest rates that I had ever paid for billing.

In fact, by converting over to this new billing company, we saved ourselves thousands of dollars annually in fees. Unfortunately, that wasn't the end of the story. Within a few years, this company started sneaking in hidden fees and rate increases, until they became so expensive that eventually I had to drop them as well. But the upside of having to go through years of frustrations with billing companies is that I was forced to learn how to handle my own billing in-house using readily available technology. My only regret is that I didn't do it sooner.

Success Strategy: *You can easily handle your own billing in-house with readily available technology. There is simply no need for billing companies any more.*

Leaving Your Current Billing Company

Interestingly enough, I later heard that some of the largest studios in the nation had dropped their old companies for lower-cost billing solutions. I can't mention the names of those schools here, but they are definitely names that you have heard and seen. I guess those huge schools decided that paying 7 to 10 times more with the traditional martial arts billing companies just wasn't worth it. Too bad for the martial arts billing and consultation companies that lost those accounts; however, if they were paying attention to their customers, that would never have happened.

The unfortunate thing about all this is that many studio owners feel like they are locked into their current billing companies. This is because many of the big martial arts billing companies will charge you a rather sizable fee if you discontinue their services and move your accounts to another company, and they usually back up their "right" to do so with a provision in their service agreement. This keeps a lot of school owners tied to companies that mistreat them and overcharge them for their services.

What these studio owners don't realize is that any contract can be broken; you just have to find the right loophole in the agreement by which to do so. Of course, this is something that you would definitely want to speak with an attorney about; I'm not in any position to give you legal advice. However, if you are getting screwed over by your current billing company and want out of their service agreement, hiring an attorney may be the only way to go. I can almost guarantee that the large schools I spoke about earlier hired an attorney or law firm to represent them when they left their old billing companies.

But, be warned; many of these large martial arts billing companies spend a considerable amount of time and effort into creating an almost cult-like atmosphere among their customers, which allows them to exert a great deal of psychological and emotional influence over their clientele. If you leave your billing company, chances are good that you will be effectively "black-balled" by that company's management and leadership. The company we left even sent "spies" into our studio to question our staff about our current operations!

So, be prepared; you will probably be bad-mouthed and lied about, and you may find out that people whom you thought to be your friends will be talking about you behind your back. This is the evil flip side to peer recognition; people will often gladly ostracize someone who does not quite fit in with their peer group, if the alpha-members of that peer group encourage them to do so. This is almost certainly because they fear falling into disfavor with their peers and becoming the object of similar treatment.

All I can tell you if you find yourself in this situation is to keep in mind that we reap what we sow. The companies and their staff that are taking advantage of people in the martial arts industry will eventually suffer the repercussions of their actions. Just keep on plowing ahead, ignore their barbs, and continue offering a great service to your clients with honesty and integrity.

In the end you will reap the positive rewards of your efforts and actions while those who have taken advantage of others are exposed for who and what they really are. If it gets really bad, you can always go hire an attorney and try suing them for slander (or libel, if they are stupid enough to actually print something that isn't true about you), but you may find that it really isn't worth the hassle and that you are better off leaving them to their own designs.

Doing Your Own Billing

In the years since I first wrote this book, billing and invoicing technology has made tremendous leaps and bounds, especially in the area of DIY billing. Despite what some billing companies are still saying, I can tell you for a certainty that it is in fact quite easy these days to do your own billing.

Now, I know that these companies will tell you that it's too much hassle, that your on-time collections will be much lower, that you don't want to be the bad guy, and that you'll still have to hire a collections agency to collect on delinquent accounts. Baloney. I've been doing my own billing for several years now, and here's what I've found with regards to these claims.

"It's a hassle to do your own billing." Maybe it was back in the days when you had to print, stuff, and stamp paper invoices each month. That was a hassle. But today? Everything is done electronically. It takes me about 60 seconds to set up a recurring billing client in our billing system. It is incredibly easy, and once it's set up, it's done – the system does the rest.

"Your on-time collections will be much lower when you do your own billing." Let me ask you something; what makes you think that the electronic billing systems the billing companies use are superior to those that are available to you? That's right, they're not – and that's because you're using the exact same technologies they use when you choose to handle your own billing. My own experiences over the last fifteen years or so have shown that your on-time collections with electronic billing systems (credit card, debit card, or bank draft) will be about 97-98%, regardless of whether you do it yourself or you hire it out to a billing company. So, why not save the extra expense and do it yourself, in-house?

"You don't want to be the bad guy." That's rich. Look, when Fat Tony the loan shark sends out Guido the enforcer to collect the vigorish on a loan, do you think that the poor sap who borrowed from Fat Tony hates him any less because it's Guido who is leaning on him? Because, quite frankly, that's about how these billing and collection companies operate, like Guido the enforcer. And guess what? They make you look like Fat Tony when they use those heavy-handed techniques to collect late payments for you. You don't want that, trust me.

Let me tell you what happens when I see that a client's scheduled payment didn't go through. When this happens I get to be the good guy, not the bad guy, and here's how. First, I call them as a courtesy and tell them that we need to update their credit card or banking information, because the payment didn't go through. Did they get a new card or change banks? I tell them I'm calling as a courtesy to save them a late fee, so we can just take care of that over the phone, or I can reschedule their payment to go through again in a few days. Typically, the client just had a rough month or maybe they had some unforeseen expenses, so just by politely calling them and rescheduling their payment it's taken care of without a fuss.

Compare that with the client getting harassing phone calls and letters from the billing company. Pretty soon, they stop answering those calls, they start associating all those negative emotions (stress) with your school, and they drop out for good. I'd say it's best if you just handle it yourself; wouldn't you agree?

"Eventually, you'll still need a collections agency." Nope, you don't, and here's why. For starters, if someone decides they don't want to pay you, there isn't much that will persuade them otherwise. In fact, you're better off calling them to find out how you dropped the ball rather than calling them to harass them for a payment. You'll get a lot more value from the first option than you will the second, believe me.

Second, the type of person who just decides to stop paying you money that they are contractually obligated to pay probably doesn't give a rip about their credit score. You can threaten them all you want about reporting them to the credit agencies, but it won't matter to them because their credit is probably already trashed.

Sure, you can take them to court. In fact, I know of a local instructor (a friend of mine, actually) who does this. He takes them to small claims court, gets a settlement, and then goes down to the county courthouse and puts a lien on the person's personal property. That means that, if they want to sell the property at some future date, they have to pay him first. Well, great. So now you're the bad guy who took someone to court and "liened up" their property because they decided little Jimmy didn't need karate lessons anymore.

Personally, I don't need that sort of bad press for my studio. This is especially true in today's world of online reputation sites and public review systems. I've seen tons of bad reviews online for martial arts schools that were simply because of a badly mishandled billing situation. Don't give someone a reason to ruin your school's reputation, just because you stubbornly want to get what's yours. For the time, energy, and money you'll spend collecting on a delinquent account, you could have just as easily gotten two or three much more clients to replace them. *Just let it go*, because it's not worth the trouble.

How to Do Your Own Billing

It's not hard. All you need is a merchant account and an online payment gateway, which you can get anywhere. Any standard merchant credit card billing account will do, and I use Authorize.net for my payment gateway as it is the most commonly used payment gateway for recurring billing purposes.

So, what you do is connect your Authorize.net payment gateway (which is like an online version of a credit card swipe machine) to your merchant account using an API login ID number and you're set.

When you want to bill someone, you just login to Authorize.net with their banking or credit card information, set up a new recurring billing profile, and you're done. Simple.

Granted, you may need some help getting all this set up at first. But I can assure you; once you get it set up it is a relatively simple way to bill your own clients.

DIY Billing Alternatives

There are several billing alternatives out there, such as PayPal, Stripe, and Google Checkout. The benefits to using one of these alternative methods is that, if you want to offer payment and registration on your website, you don't have to mess with PCI compliance and other regulatory hassles. I suggest that you explore all your options before settling on a primary electronic billing method.

Contracts: Should You Use Them?

I am a big proponent of using contracts in your studio. The reasons for this are manifold, but I will list the most important ones here:

1. **Legal Protection** - By laying out in detail exactly what services you will provide to your clients and in what manner, a good contract can act to protect you if you are ever sued by a client in a court of law. By clarifying your relationship with your clients at the get-go, you will prevent confusion later on as to what you did and did not promise them when they enrolled. Trust me; you need to use contracts if only for this reason.

2. **Increased Rates of Collection** – Some people are more apt to pay their bills when they know that they can be turned in to the credit bureaus for paying late or for non-payment. I know this sounds harsh, but it's a fact of

life. There is a certain type of client that you will get in your studio who will always pay late and be behind on their tuition. Sometimes, only the threat of sending them to a collection agency will make them pay (it doesn't mean you have to do it, but the threat of it is often enough to get them to settle their account with you). Of course, some people don't care at all and will default regardless, but that's no reason to just write off all your slow-pays and no-pays for good. Getting some money is better than getting none at all.

3. **Discouraging Drop Outs** – Americans are fickle, and their kids are doubly so. One month they want to be the next Bruce Lee, the next they lose interest, and the next they are training again as hard as ever. It is up to you as their instructor to hold them responsible for the commitment they have made to you, and to teach them to follow through on their goals. What kind of message are you sending about your own estimation of the value of your time and effort, when you allow your students to come and go as they please? Using membership agreements helps create an atmosphere where the student is aware that you as their instructor expect a serious commitment from them, and it also informs the student that you will hold them to their word. The value of teaching your students accountability and perseverance in this manner cannot be overstated.

While some school owners decry the use of membership agreements and claim to be doing fine without them, I believe that they are doing themselves and their students a tremendous disservice by not using them. I wholeheartedly recommend that you use them in your studio, and that you hold your clients accountable for their financial obligation to your business. Anything less is not only bad business, it's just unfair to you and the rest of your students.

Important Point: *Contracts do more than just lock-in your clients. They should be an effective and integral part of your overall risk-management plan. In addition, they assist you in creating a "culture" of commitment in your studio.*

Explaining the Membership Agreement

It is extremely important that you explain and disclose the terms of your contract to a prospective client immediately before they sign it. Failing to do so will nullify the contract at the very least, and in a worst-case scenario it can get you into serious hot water with the authorities in some states. Before the client signs, be sure to explain the following major points to them in plain English:

- The fact that they have to pay regardless of whether or not they attend classes. We always tell our clients that our memberships are just like gym memberships; even if you don't go to the gym to work out, you still have to pay your monthly dues. Most everyone understands this requirement when it is explained in this fashion.
- The length of the agreement.
- The amount of their monthly payments and when they are due each month.
- The number of payments they will have to make.
- The total cost of the membership, including an explanation of any additional fees.
- When late fees will be assessed to their account if they pay late.
- How much the finance charges are that are being assessed on their balance and the annual percentage rate of interest. If you decide to charge interest be sure that it is allowed by law in your state and stay within the limits

set by law for the Annual Percentage Rate. I never charged interest on a membership balance, but you might decide to do so; personally, I think it just complicates things and is not worth the extra money.

- Any other pertinent details relating to their membership and financial obligation.

Important Point: *Explain the details of your agreement to avoid complications later on down the road.*

The old adage, "A stitch in time saves nine" applies well here. Just be sure to be honest and be thorough when explaining the agreement and you will avoid complications down the road when a client pays late or wants to drop out. But by all means, do not allow a client to sign their membership agreement unless you have explained the terms and conditions to them beforehand.

Now, on to the next chapter where I will cover one of my favorite subjects - Marketing on a Budget!

TEN

MARKETING ON A BUDGET

What Is Marketing?

The American Marketing Association defines marketing as "the process of planning and executing the conception, pricing, promotion, and distribution of ideas, goods, and services to create exchanges that satisfy individual and organizational objectives." What this long dry definition means to us is this; marketing is an integral and necessary part of our studio operations. Without it, we will fail or be destined to spend the rest of our careers in a hell of mediocrity and "should-have-been." In other words: No marketing = no customers = no money = no studio.

Our **goals** in marketing our martial arts studio are:

- **To bring in new leads/customers** (our short-term goal),
- **To educate the public on our services** (our mid-term goal), and
- **To firmly position ourselves as <u>the</u> expert and**

leader on the martial arts within our communities (our long-term goal).

These three important goals must be retained as our guiding doctrine when approaching the formulation of our overall marketing plan. A comprehensive marketing plan includes the "four P's" of marketing: Product, Price, Promotion, and Place (delivery of the good or service to the consumer). Since we have already covered Product, Price, and Place in other sections of this manual, let's discuss the most relevant aspect or our overall marketing plan: Promotion.

An Important Aspect of Marketing: Promotion

In marketing terminology, **promotion** is the process of conveying information and ideas about a product to the consumer with the intent of swaying consumer opinion in favor of the product, thereby increasing demand for that product. While promotion is really just 25% of an overall marketing plan, it is the area that we are going to concentrate on most heavily in this chapter.

Before I go any further into this section, let me define a few terms for you so you can understand the big picture in marketing your studio. **Promotion** is a combination of **personal selling, mass selling**, and **sales promotion**. Personal selling is when you are directly in conversation with a potential client with the purpose of influencing that client to purchase your product, a subject that we covered in some detail in the chapter on pricing. Mass selling is when you are communicating with a large number of potential clients through some **advertising medium**, such as television, newspapers, radio, signs, direct mail, and the like, or through **publicity**, which is any unpaid non-personal presentation of your service. **Sales promotions** are things you do to sell your services other than advertising, publicity and personal selling. Some examples of sales promotions are contests, coupons, customer referral programs, and offering free gifts with a purchase (such as a free uniform).

The following diagram will help you understand how the different aspects of promotion fit together:

We will cover different aspects of promotion throughout this chapter. While we will not necessarily cover them in order, you may find it helpful to become familiar with the diagram above so you can identify where each aspect of promotion fits into your overall marketing plan.

Marketing Success Starts with a Plan

By now, you know how I feel about planning in your business, and marketing is no exception. Without a good marketing plan, you will be shooting in the dark as far as your marketing efforts go, and you will likely waste a considerable amount of money with no measurable results to show for it. Of course, planning your marketing does take time and effort, but you will be rewarded admirably for your investment.

But, what makes a good marketing plan? Well, for starters a good marketing plan must exhibit the following characteristics:

1. **It must be logical.** Just guessing at how you are going to market your product or service is wasteful and foolish; you must take the time to examine your target market or consumers, and learn their needs, their wants, and how they spend their money. In this way you can direct your efforts accordingly.

2. **It must be measurable.** If you use a marketing method that is not measurable, how will you know if it works? In answer to this question, you might be thinking, "Well, when the customers show up." That's fine if you are only using one method of advertisement, but chances are good that you will be using several different advertising methods. Having the ability to measure which ones are most successful will enable you to redirect your advertising dollars and efforts to those methods that show the greatest return on investment.

3. **It must be practical to implement.** If your marketing plan is too time-intensive or money-intensive to implement, what good is it? Your marketing plan must be practical, and fit within your budget and the limits of your available resources.

4. **It must be directed to the desired audience.** It won't do you much good to advertise your school in a national magazine, although I see this done all the time. Even if you get students from running a national ad, it's like using a sledgehammer to kill a fly. Make your advertising dollars and efforts count by keeping them focused on your target audience.

5. **And, it must be adaptable to changing times.** Your marketing plan must be flexible. Oftentimes you will find that some methods work better during certain times of the year, or that an ad that has pulled impressive numbers for months suddenly isn't doing well, or that your marketing costs have gone up due to inflation and

increases in the cost of doing business. Also, with the advent of new technologies, you will want to have the leeway to be able to test new marketing methods as they come available. You need to have a flexible marketing plan that you can quickly change to adapt to differing circumstances.

You should constantly and continually assess your marketing plan versus the above criteria to ensure that it does not grow stale or become ineffectual over time.

Success Strategy: *Continually reassess your marketing plan for effectiveness, and be willing to revise the plan if necessary. Remember, you are not married to any one method or approach to marketing.*

Consistency: One of the Keys to Marketing Success

Once you have a good marketing plan worked out, you must take action to implement it and see it through. You should also be consistent in your marketing efforts! One of the worst mistakes that a business owner can make is to be inconsistent in their marketing efforts.

Results come from marketing momentum, and that takes time to build. The last thing you want to do is to build up momentum with your marketing plan, experience a sudden surge in business, and then back off on your marketing efforts. If you do, you will have wasted all of the time and resources you spent in building up the momentum that it took to get you to that point. So, once you start seeing results from your efforts, you need to be consistent and keep plugging away with your marketing plan.

Success Strategy: Be consistent in your marketing efforts.

The Three Areas of Marketing Focus

For martial arts schools, there are three areas of marketing focus:

- **Internal marketing:** Internal marketing has to do with educating and informing your current clients about additional products and services that they might purchase in your school, thereby increasing your bottom line. Internal marketing also entails using special promotions to get new client referrals from your existing members; this approach of harvesting customer referrals is a powerful marketing resource that should be an integral part of your overall marketing plan.
- **External marketing:** External marketing consists of paid and free advertisements outside your studio walls that are designed to attract new clients into your studio and to educate the public on your services. You will be spending 80-90% of your overall advertising budget and efforts here, so make it count!
- **Public relations:** Strictly speaking, the term "public relations" ("PR") refers to communicating with non-customers. For our purposes, however, the focus of PR is to make community contacts and appearances in order to improve the public's perception of your business. This area of marketing is often overlooked and even completely ignored by small business owners; yet, it is one of the most effective means of making sure that your advertising dollars don't go to waste. Creating good PR is time-intensive, but well worth the effort, because it

generally doesn't cost anything other than your time to create.

All of your marketing efforts will fall within these three classifications or areas. Your marketing plan should be balanced between the three, although at first you may find yourself focusing more on external marketing or public relations due to the rapid results these areas often get in bringing in new clients. As your clientele grows, you can then increase your efforts in the area of internal marketing for higher profits and increased customer referrals for your studio.

A Universal Marketing Cost Axiom

Once you begin developing your marketing plan, you will likely notice something peculiar about marketing that has perplexed me for years. There is a peculiar phenomenon regarding the cost and effort involved in various methods of marketing. Where cost and effort are concerned, all marketing methods will fall in either one of two categories:

- High-cost, but low-effort
- Low-cost, but high-effort

I have yet to see a low-cost marketing method that requires little effort to implement; although some methods are touted as such (such as bulk e-mail) they never quite work out that way. But, this is good news, because when you are first starting out you may find that you have more time than money. For the cost of a little sweat and time, you can actually market your business effectively without spending a whole lot of cash to do so. So, pay attention to the low-cost marketing methods that follow and formulate your plan accordingly.

How Many Promotions & Events Should You Do?

Some small business owners think that just using one form of advertisement and keeping it going year round is enough. Nope! You need to be marketing in all three areas using many different advertisement channels every month.

In his book, "How to Make Millions with Your Ideas," marketing great Dan Kennedy quotes a highly successful chiropractor and client he worked with as saying, "I do not know of one way to obtain 100 new patients. But I do know of 100 ways to get one new patient, so I use them all." While most of your marketing promotions will bring in a whole lot more than one new client, having multiple promotions going on at once acts to hedge your bets against the possibility that one method may falter. Accordingly, it simply makes good business sense to do so.

Important Point: Your chief marketing goal is to get a minimum of 24 fresh new leads each month. To accomplish this, you should run a minimum of 2 internal marketing promotions, 3 external marketing promotions, and 1 public relations event every month.

These are the bare minimum numbers that you should follow to ensure that you are doing enough to keep your business in the public eye and to keep new clients coming in year round. You want to keep your marketing momentum going at all times. Use your marketing budget guideline of spending 10% of your gross income on your marketing every month and stick to the above numbers when planning monthly promotions and you will achieve and maintain marketing momentum. Also, planning events well in advance will make this a whole lot easier to do.

Important Point: Plan ahead! Have your marketing promotions planned out by the middle of the month for the upcoming month.

Building a Marketing Funnel in the Digital Era...

When I first wrote this book, you could still get good results from traditional print advertising methods like news ads and the yellow pages, and digital (online) marketing was still in its infancy. Back then, there really wasn't a need to set up and manage a sophisticated marketing funnel for a small business; you just placed an ad in the newspaper or yellow pages, and then waited for the calls to come in. However, within just a few short years digital media has crowded out the traditional mass media channels (print, radio, and television), making those methods nearly obsolete for our marketing purposes.

Advances in data transmission and mobile technology have led to the creation of multiple digital marketing channels, all clamoring for your customer's attention. This means that your market is being bombarded 24/7 with distractions that detract from their ability to focus on one single marketing message, which has had the net effect of creating a populace that suffers from digital attention deficit disorder. And, although it has never been easier to get your marketing message out to your target audience (because we have more marketing channels at our disposal than ever, and many of them free), it also has never been harder to get your target audience to *pay attention* to your message.

This is why print advertising is merely an afterthought in marketing today, and why online marketing has taken the front and center position in every small business owner's marketing plan. Let me be clear – you *must* market your business online if you want to grow your studio. And, because online marketing changes so rapidly, you have to stay on top of trends in digital marketing in order to stay ahead of your competition.

Currently, there are numerous online marketing channels to choose from, including getting good search engine results and buying search engine ads for your website ("search engine optimization" and "pay-per-click advertising"), social media marketing, blogging, online video marketing, podcasting, article marketing; the list is endless. However, there is one thing that remains constant in the realm of marketing a martial arts studio; that is, you need a clear marketing message (well-written sales copy) and you need a way to get that message in front of your target audience. How you do that is going to change from time to time due to trends and changes in online marketing, but the basic approach is the same. *You need to build a marketing funnel.*

To do this, my suggestion is that you start with your website, which will be the "fill point" for your marketing funnel (see the illustration on the following page). Make sure that you have a website that is designed for direct response marketing; one that is made specifically for the purpose of generating leads (email leads or phone calls). Use an autoresponder service to collect and manage email leads (and to follow up automatically), and hire a good copywriter to write your home page sales copy or learn how to write good copy yourself. You want your site to be set up so that your site visitors are compelled to either call you or to fill out a lead capture form on the site. So focus on crafting a phenomenal and compelling message, because good copywriting is what sells online.

Once the site is set up you are going to start driving traffic to it using a combination of free and paid traffic generation methods. Free traffic methods include search engine optimization (SEO), social media marketing, video marketing (posting videos on free video websites that direct viewers to your site), article marketing, and blogging. Paid traffic sources include pay-per-click ads, social media ads, and paid placement ads on local high-traffic websites. Using a combination of these paid and free traffic methods, your goal is to get enough traffic to your website to generate a *minimum* of 15 leads a month (but don't stop there – I know of martial art schools that get 50 or more leads a month from their website).

Then, once you have your website set up and cranking out leads, you should start working on expanding your marketing to include some offline marketing methods *in order to drive more visitors to your website*. Everything should point to your website, and the point of your entire marketing plan should be to funnel people to your site. That's because your website is the only place where you can completely control and deliver your marketing message without any distractions, and where you stand the best chance of capturing that lead.

As for which offline marketing methods to use, I am partial to guest passes, door hangers, and snipe signs (also known as political signs or yard signs) because these methods have worked well for me over the years. However, I know school owners who use various other methods, such as school talks, lead boxes, take ones (postcards that are like a compact brochure, with an offer and a call-to-action), and even print ads in select publications. However, I suggest you start with guest passes and door hangers because they are both effective and economical.

Specific Marketing Methods

Now that I've explained how to set up your marketing funnel, let's move on and examine various marketing methods that fall under each of the three areas that your marketing plan will cover, so you can have a more thorough understanding of the specific ways in which you can market your business. I have denoted each method's approximate cost and the effort involved, thereby making it easier for you to target your marketing efforts in the beginning when you don't have much money. We'll start with...

External Marketing

There are countless ways in which you can advertise externally. I will list some of the most common and some uncommon methods and explain how to use each most effectively.

- **Websites (cost: low to high, depending on whether you do it yourself or hire someone; time & effort: low to high, once again depending on whether you do it yourself or hire someone)** – Since I first wrote this book more than a decade ago, websites have gone from a "nice to have" to a "must have" marketing component. Done properly, your website will be the central marketing tool in your arsenal that will bring in the bulk of your leads; done wrong, it will be a major waste of your time, effort, and money. The first thing I am going to tell you about building a site for your school is to ignore and forget whatever any web designer or web programmer tells you that you need on your site. They tend to get hung up on pretty design and including slick functions that don't really help you get leads. Instead, you need a good direct marketing website, one that is focused on good sales copy (and remember, you can use video to deliver your sales content as well). So, **you need a multi-page website** (typically this will include a sales letter or video on your home page, a contact us page, an about us page, and a sales page for each of your programs or target audiences), a means of collecting contact information on every page of your site, a great web address that is easy to remember and will help you rank well in the search engines, and of course some decent sales copy to make your site a 24-hour leads machine. You also need to have your site optimized for good search engine ranking by an SEO specialist who knows what they're doing. I've written about web marketing extensively on my blog at MartialArtsBusinessDaily.com; go there and search the site for "web marketing", "websites", "online marketing", and so on for more information on getting your website done right.

Success Strategy: Once you get your site set up properly, no one will go there unless you tell them how to get to it. Put your web address on everything you put out; ads, business cards, fliers, mailers, coupons, your social media profiles, in your email signature, and anywhere else you can think of where people will see it.

- **Social Media (cost: low; time & effort: high)** – My, how times have changed. Again, when I first wrote this book, hardly anyone knew what social media was; now it's everywhere. Yes, you need to use social media marketing. Rather than provide you with a bunch of information here that will likely be outdated in six months or a year, instead I suggest that you visit MartialArtsBusinessDaily.com and do a search on "social media marketing" for the most recent articles I've written dealing with this topic.

- **Online Classifieds Websites** (cost: low; time & effort: moderate) – This is an advertising method that many people overlook, but one that can bring in a consistent lead flow for your studio. The great thing about using these sites (currently, the most popular site is Craigslist, but there are many others as well) is that they are free or very nearly free to use. The only downside is that you need to spend time running a few new ads every day of the week to get results. The best way to do this is to write unique ad content and headlines every day of the week, and then use html code to insert an image into your ads that will display the actual marketing message, and that will link to (or direct the reader to visit) your website. If you are unfamiliar with writing html code, you can easily find someone to do this for you. The good news is that once you have the html code, you can use the same ad over and over by simply changing the headline and wording in the description for the ad. Also, be sure to use keywords like "martial arts" and your city name in your ads, since this can often result in those ads being picked up by the search engines. One final note: *Do not* use software that automatically posts your ads; it will get you banned from these sites.

- **Online Business Directories (cost, free to moderate; time & effort, low to moderate)** – These directories are too numerous to name, but you mainly want to focus on getting listed in the Google business directory. This is a must; hire someone who is proficient in search engine marketing to help you with this if you are not very web savvy. A good SEO specialist can also ensure that your business gets listed in all the other major online directories as well.

- **Pay-Per-Click Search Engine Advertising** – Pay-per-click ads (also known as PPC) can help you quickly get more traffic to your site. Setting up a campaign properly can be technically challenging though, so be prepared to either spend many frustrating hours figuring it out, or to spend some money on an SEO specialist who understands how to set up local PPC campaigns. Speaking of which, make sure that you are only advertising in your local area; I've seen a lot of studios waste money on advertising outside of their immediate area, simply because their campaigns were set up wrong. Again, hire someone to help you with this if you are not web savvy.

- **Print ads (cost: moderate to high; time & effort: low)** – Print ads are advertisements that you place in periodicals, such as your local newspaper, monthly magazines, and newsletters. Print ads can be a very effective component of your advertising plan if you use a good ad in the right publication (we'll be covering the elements of an effective ad in a minute). In larger cities, however, running print ads can easily eat up your entire marketing budget. As far as ad size goes, a well-designed 2 column by 6-inch ad should be more than large enough to attract attention in most papers and magazines; however, if you can afford it, a larger size ad is more likely to be seen. Whatever the case, make sure that you buy enough ad space to get noticed, but not so much that you can't afford to do any other advertising. Also, be sure that the publication you advertise in has enough circulation (the number of copies distributed per issue) and readership (the number of people who actually read the darn thing) to merit your spending money to advertise in it. If you advertise in the largest local newspaper whenever possible this shouldn't be a problem. Like I said before, publications like the "Penny Saver," "The Thrifty Nickel," and other weekly shoppers are unlikely to pull the type of inquiries that you want; however, you may try them for a month just to test how they do in your area. Final note: Even after I started relying on web marketing for most of my lead generation, I still kept a 2 column by 5 inch print ad running continually in my local paper simply for the name recognition and exposure it gave me.

- **The Yellow Pages (cost: moderate to high; time & effort: low)** – The Yellow Pages are almost completely irrelevant these days. Just get a free listing, and don't waste money paying for their online listings or custom lead generation services either; you don't need them and the ROI (return on investment) is not worth the cost.

- **Television (cost: moderate to high; time & effort: low)** – This method is generally too costly for the return you get on your investment. For starters, it will cost you $300 to $1,500 just to purchase or produce a basic 30-second commercial (and there's no guarantee that what you get will pull for you). Then, in order for your commercial to be effective, you will need it to air frequently so people will see it. Besides that, you can post your own video "commercials" for free on YouTube now, and you'll probably get better results from it as well. So unless you get a heck of a good deal, I don't recommend using TV. However, we will discuss using the TV and radio in other less costly ways when we get to the PR section.

- **Radio** – Ditto on everything I said about television.
- **Direct Mail (cost: moderate to high; time & effort: moderate)** – Tricky, but effective. If you want to use this method successfully, you will need to design an eye-catching mailing piece, compile or rent a good, targeted list to mail to, and follow up on a regular basis with more mailings. You can get good targeted mailing lists from InfoUSA (http://www.infousa.com). They now have neighborhood mass mailing lists, so you can target specific areas that are close to your school with your direct mail campaign. There is not enough space in this manual to explain how to run an effective direct mail campaign; I suggest you read up on how to use direct mail to market your business before dipping your toes in these waters.
- **Coupon Mailers (cost: low to moderate; time & effort: low)** – I listed this method separately from direct mail because I don't feel that they are in the same league. While coupon-mailing services such as Val-Pak are often considered to be direct mail, they don't have the same potential for success as a standalone mailing so I wanted to be sure that I was clear on this distinction. In the past I had used Val-Pak with some degree of success in my own studio, but more recently results have been mixed. If you decide to test this marketing method, do so with caution.

Important Point: Don't make the mistake of assuming that graphic artists and webpage designers are experts on marketing. While they may be able to design a pretty ad or website, they usually don't know squat about making it effective for pulling customers.

- **Flier Distribution and Door Hangers (cost: low to moderate; time and effort: high)** – Over the years I have become quite fond of door-to-door flier marketing, because it is cheap and highly effective if you have a good flier or door hanger. In fact, I have found this method to be effective as or even more effective than direct mail. The bad news is that there may be restrictions on its usage in your area, and unless you do it yourself, you never know what the guy who is delivering the piece house-to-house will look like. (One school owner I know stopped using this method after he got a call from someone who had received his flier at their house. Apparently, the distribution service was using day laborers to deliver his pieces, and one of them relieved himself at the lady's front door!) While I think door-to-door flier and door hanger distribution is a good way to advertise, I advise you to make sure that you use a reputable company with all the proper credentials and permits. Of course, you can distribute fliers yourself door-to-door, and also by placing them on public bulletin boards and anywhere else you can think of where people will see them. When using this method, the key is to have an eye-catching ad, with a great offer. Always include a highly visible coupon with a time limit for redemption at the bottom, as it generally increases response rates.
- **Billboards (cost: high; time & effort: low)** – This will only work if you can find billboard space close to your studio. This method can be cost-prohibitive to use, so if it is going to eat up most of your advertising budget to get a billboard done, skip it entirely. But, if you

find a billboard close to your studio and if you can get a
reasonable rate, it's not a bad way to go for exposure.
Make sure that the sign is located on a main thoroughfare
and not on some obscure road that no one uses. Also,
follow the rules I list later in this chapter when designing
your ad. Since most people will only be able to read a few
words as they drive by, keep the ad copy simple and limit
it to a bold, eye-catching headline, your school name,
phone number, and possibly your web address at the
bottom of the ad. Remember, use colors that contrast well
with each other for your background and lettering.

- **Your Street Sign (cost: over the course of your
  business life, low, but initially high; time &
  effort: very low)** – You need to have the largest street
  sign that your local zoning laws and landlord will allow.
  Use large red or black letters and a block font like Arial
  Black or Franklin Gothic Heavy with a white
  background for visibility; fancy layouts, fonts, and color
  schemes will just be a waste of money because no one
  will be able to read it. As with the billboard, keep it short
  and simple. If your school name is long or confusing, just
  put "KARATE", "KUNG-FU", "JIU JITSU", or "SELF-
  DEFENSE" in big letters at the top of the sign; people
  recognize these names much better than terms such as
  "fu jow pai," "tae kwon do," and other more obscure
  martial arts monikers. If the sign is big enough, you can
  always list what you teach in bullets below the heading.
  The most important thing to remember is to list your
  phone number *and web address* prominently on the sign;
  in fact, it should take up at least 1/4 of the sign space.
- **Brochures (cost: very low to low; time &
  effort: low to moderate)** – You should have a nice,
  professional looking brochure printed up for your studio.
  If you don't have the graphic design know-how to make

one yourself, get with your local printer and have them do it for you. Unless you are just starting out, do not put out brochures that have been printed on your printer at home (same goes for business cards). Once you can afford them, get your brochures professionally printed. Now, as for what goes in a brochure, you need to explain your programs from the viewpoint of the customer ("what's in it for me?"). When you write your brochure you can gloss over facts, and instead mostly focus your ad copy on the benefits that the client will experience in taking your program (this goes for all ad copy). Be sure that your logo is prominently displayed on the brochure, and include some pictures of people from your classes having fun while training. Do not use pictures of people getting beat up, unless you are teaching a self-defense oriented program and the picture is of a much smaller, weaker person defending himself or herself against a much larger attacker that is obviously the "bad guy." Place a brochure holder on the outside wall next to the entrance of your studio. Fill it with brochures whenever you are not open so people can get info on your classes. Be sure to empty the holder when you open the studio each day; otherwise, people may take a brochure without coming in.

Success Strategy: Remember, people like facts, but they buy benefits. Include both in your ads.

Other, Less Common Methods of Advertising

- **Banner Signs (cost: low to moderate; time & effort: low)** – Banners swing and move, so they tend to draw attention. If allowed by the zoning laws in your area, you should have a different banner in front of your school every month, preferably right on the street where all the passing cars can see it. Same rules go for banner design as for your street sign, except black letters on a yellow background also work well if the banner is close to the street; if it is more than 20 feet from the road, use red, darker blue, and black letters on a white background. The most effective way to use banners is to advertise your promotions on them. Also, be sure to use a banner size that will allow for lettering that can be seen at a distance.

- **Snipe Signs (cost: low to moderate; time & effort: high)** – Snipe signs, sometimes called bandit signs or campaign signs, are a very effective and low-cost means of advertising when used properly. I am sure that you have seen them used in your area; they are those little signs on the side of the road that look like real estate "house for sale" signs. If your local regulations allow, putting out 50-100 signs printed with a simple message like "Kid's Karate 555-5555 YourCityKidsKarate.com" can bring in a ton of business for you. Always try to place them at the corner of a major intersection on the **right hand side** of the road, in groups of two or three spaced about 15-20 feet apart just off the shoulder of the road. You can order them online in bundles of 100 for about a $2.00 a piece, with wire frames. Plan on replacing them about once a month; just figure it into your advertising budget. Oh, and if you're like me and live in a town that has some pretty Draconian laws with regards to sidewalk and right-of-way signage, you can offer your students a discount on tuition or a free uniform for placing a snipe sign in their yard. I know, it sounds crazy, but I guarantee that some of your people will take you up on the offer.

- **Lead Boxes and "Take Ones" (cost: low to**

moderate; time & effort: high) – I have spoken with several studio owners that do quite well using this method. It does require some work to be effective, but it is great for studios on a budget. There are numerous businesses that sell lead boxes and take ones that are specifically designed for martial arts studios. My suggestion is that you have them custom printed with your school's contact information, and that you start by placing them in a minimum of 25 locations within a three to five mile radius of your studio. And if you can manage it, 100 locations would be even better. Be sure to check them every week, as they tend to get destroyed, thrown away, and vandalized quite regularly.

- **Pizza Boxes (cost: low; time & effort: moderate**) – I know, it sounds weird, but I have a friend who swears by this method. He pays a minuscule amount per piece to have his fliers attached to pizza boxes by the local pizza delivery place. None of the major franchises in my local area would agree to do this for us, but you may have different results; call around and speak with the managers at your local pizza parlors to see if they'd be willing to let you do this.

Internal Marketing

Many studio owners fail to see the need to market within their own studios. However, internal marketing allows you to get more benefits out of the client base you already have. This will lead to more profit, more referrals, and more satisfied customers. As well as being a crucial aspect of your overall marketing plan, internal promotions should be an integral component of your retention system as well. Do not overlook this part of your marketing.

Internal marketing consists of creating reasons for your customers to both spend more money at your studio and to bring in new student referrals. An internal marketing event can be geared toward one or both of these goals. We will discuss different internal marketing events later on in the section on multiple profit centers; for now, I will focus on a few key strategies that you should use on an ongoing basis to get new customer referrals from your clients.

- **Guest passes (cost: low; time & effort: moderate to high)** – Guest passes are one of the best ways for you to get a steady stream of referrals from your clients. You can design your guest passes however you like; I use a business card-sized pass imprinted with the following information on the front: "Guest Pass! This card is good for one FREE MONTH of martial arts classes at ABC KARATE. Call us at 555-5555 or stop by our studio at 123 Main Street in Anytown, Texas to schedule your first class." In small letters at the bottom they said, "Offer good for new students only. Maximum redeemable value of card is $150.00." On the back, I had the following printed on the card: "This card is for _____. Compliments of _____. Call us at 555-5555 to schedule your first lesson!" These cards could only be given out by our members and staff; we kept a constant supply of them on display in our studio so students could give them out whenever they wanted. However, in order to eliminate people taking advantage of us, we asked our students and staff to only give them to people that they thought would make good students. While you may think giving away a free month of classes is a mistake, I can assure you that it is a lot cheaper than you think. When a prospect brought in one of these cards, we offered a 50% discount to the student on their uniform and gave them their free month; although it may seem like we were "losing" a month's tuition, we were actually getting a new student for the cost of one business card! Compared to spending $50 or more per lead to generate inquiries, this is quite a bargain. So long as you are teaching great classes, you are following up on the new prospects, and you are encouraging them to enroll before their month is up (we offer to waive their membership fee if they enroll before the end of their free month) you will get a new student from 90% of the Guest Passes that come back to you. I highly recommend this method – it's cheap and it works.

- **Guest Contests (cost: low to moderate; time & effort: moderate to high)** – This is a way of taking your guest pass program to the next level. A few times a year, you simply make it known that you will give some sort of prize to students who refer a certain number of new students to the school. For instance, two referrals might be worth a school t-shirt, five might be worth a student uniform, and ten might be good for a free private lesson with the instructor. Offer a grand prize for the student that refers the most new students before the end of the contest. Whatever the reward, make sure that it is something that your students will like and that you keep track of the referrals and follow through on giving out the prizes. Make a poster and fliers that explain the program, and post them prominently in your studio where your students can see them. Announce the contest at the end of each class, and give prizes out in front of the other students, maybe at a special event like graduation night. Using this method will send your referrals through the roof.

- **Special Events (cost: low to moderate; time & effort: high)** – Special events include seminars, workshops, parties, graduations, and other events that attract people into your school who normally would never walk through your front door. These can be free events, or events that you charge a fee to attend. However, I can tell you from experience that there is nothing that can build your enrollment faster than offering free women's self-defense and child safety workshops in your area. Again, this is a topic that I have written about extensively on my blog. Visit MartialArtsBusinessDaily.com and search on "women's self defense" and "child safety" for more information on this topic.

That just about everything you need to know to get started on the internal and external promotion aspects of your marketing plan. Now, we are going to discuss an area of marketing that most studio owners overlook to their own detriment: Public Relations!

Public Relations

"The consent of the public is basic to the success of any venture."
  - Thomas Jefferson

Public relations campaigns are perhaps the most under-utilized method of marketing in the martial arts industry. Yet, if you asked around at successful schools, I bet you would discover that a high percentage of them use public relations events on a regular basis to get exposure for their studios. In every instance that I am aware of where a studio implemented a comprehensive PR campaign, that studio experienced phenomenal growth within the next twelve-month period. If you want to be successful and be known as the expert in your community, get working on a public relations campaign and start implementing it immediately.

Formulating and implementing a good PR campaign takes time and effort; the great news is that it will not cost you much to do so. In addition, I don't think that there is another area of marketing in which you can experience such phenomenal results from your efforts; this makes the time and effort you invest well worth it. But, it can also be more involved than any other method. Study the following instructions in detail before you embark on your public relations effort to ensure that you get the most from your efforts.

First Things First: Your Professional Image

Putting forth a professional image is perhaps the most important prerequisite to starting a public relations campaign that I can think of. Let me put it to you bluntly; if your campaign works and you get lots of attention from the press and community but you look like Backwards Bubba from the Bayou your efforts will have been for nothing because no one will take you seriously.

All idealism aside, society *will* judge you on your outward appearance. So, let's go over various aspects of your professional image that you must address in order that you should present yourself favorably to the press and public:

- **Your Personal Appearance** – Your personal image is extremely important! This includes your clothing, your manner of speech, your hairstyle, and your figure. You may not like to hear this, but listen up; if you are overweight, very few people will be likely to take you seriously as a competent, professional martial artist. Now, I have seen some hefty folks that could really perform their art well; regardless, in marketing we have to look at things from the public's viewpoint. The public is used to seeing fit, trim, buff martial artists on TV and in the movies; if you're overweight, the average person is going to look at you and think, "Chris Farley, Beverly Hills

Ninja." Stay trim to improve your professional image. Also, no facial hair and no outrageous clothing or hair styles. No facial or body piercing, and cover up your tattoos. While these forms of "personal expression" have come into vogue in recent years, you want to appeal as much as possible to mainstream society, and the fact is you won't accomplish that if you walk around all day looking like a fan at a thrash metal concert. Trust me; keep your image as clean cut as possible and it will pay off.

- **Your Manner of Dress** – Once again, go mainstream. Read up on this, and learn how to present a professional image. Also, check out how your target market dresses, and dress like they do.

- **Your Manner of Speech** – Use proper grammar and avoid slang. By all means, no foul language! Also, avoid speaking poorly of other instructors and styles; this will only serve to make you look petty and insignificant in the eyes of others (think of Stone in the movie "Sidekicks"). Improve your vocabulary by listening to tapes and reading books designed for that purpose. Don't be fake; just be better.

- **Your Car** – You may not drive the nicest or newest ride in the neighborhood (yet) but you can at least keep it clean and well maintained. If you have to go to an important event or meeting and you drive a clunker, borrow a nicer car from someone else or get a ride.

- **Your Stationary and Letterhead** – You are going to be sending out a lot of letters and handing out a lot of business cards; you need to be sure that they look good. The other day, as I came across my very first business card in an old box in my closet I had to laugh out loud. It was tacky and unprofessional, and just screamed "amateur!" Your printed materials should look like they came from a large, high-priced law firm or from the desk of a corporate executive. Here are some suggestions as to how you should design your stationary, business cards, and letterhead:

✓ **Business Cards** – Thick card stock in white or off-white, and preferably in a linen or parchment pattern; subdued colors, nothing too bright or gaudy; raised or engraved lettering if you can afford it; gold or silver ink for your logo and business name if you can afford it; and they should match your letterhead and stationary. **Do not** use generic designs or print them yourself at home.

✓ **Letterhead** - Custom layout done by you or your graphic artist; linen or parchment paper that matches your business cards down to the ink color and fonts; display your logo in the upper left hand corner; your school name at the top with your contact information tastefully displayed underneath or at the bottom of the page; spare, minimalist design; nothing garish, no bright colors.

✓ **Stationary** – Should match your letterhead and business cards.

• **Your School** – Clean, neat, well kept. School name, phone number, and hours of operation posted in neat vinyl lettering on the door (get your sign shop to do this). Get an interior designer to help you pick walls colors and flooring (I've seen some schools pattern their design after Starbucks, and that's also a good look). Potted plants in key places; nice, tasteful wall hangings. Well-lighted and devoid of that "locker-room" odor; use light bulbs that simulate sunlight, get an ozone-producing air purifier and use an odor eliminator every day when cleaning the studio. Also, get your carpets professionally cleaned once a month. Keep your mats sanitized as well. Your restroom should be spotless; as clean as your bathroom at home (bachelors: as clean as your mom's bathroom). Clean glass and mirrors (but, I think mirrors are a waste of money and they distract young children; you don't need them so don't buy them if you are just starting out). Basically, a studio that any professional would feel comfortable training in.

- **Your Students** – Implement a uniform dress code, and enforce it. Make it a requirement for promotion that students have the proper uniform; clean, neat, odor and stain-free, with all required patches in the right place and sewn on by a professional service. Proper etiquette at all times. Discipline and respect, always.

Using Press Releases to Generate Positive Press

The press release is perhaps the single most powerful tool you have for the purposes of generating favorable press coverage for your studio. However, if done improperly sending out press releases can sink your chances of getting any coverage by your local press. You must be sure to use the correct approach when issuing a press release to avoid irritating your press contacts.

There is a certain method of approaching members of the press that will enable you to get in their good graces. The first thing is to send out the press release in the proper format, typed neatly using correct spelling and grammar, and addressed to the right person or department. If you send a press release describing your upcoming tournament to the business editor, chances are good that it will go in her circular file. Take the time to find out who the editor is in the department pertaining to your story, and address the release directly to that person.

The next step is to politely follow up. Be as courteous as possible when phoning to follow up on your press release. Just tell the person you are speaking with that you sent a press release to them earlier in the week, and you were just calling to see if they received it. If they didn't, offer to send another copy. If they did, great, thank them for their time, and hang up; do not ask if they are going to run a story based on your press release and don't call them again until you send out another release on a different story. If they want to run a story on your event, they will let you know.

Also, don't be discouraged if you send out several press releases and don't get a story written on any of them; be patient, be polite, be persistent and they will come. Writers always have a need for assistance with research and people to interview, and if you've been consistent with sending out your press releases, when it comes time for them to write a martial arts related story they'll be calling you. Once again, remember that patience and being polite will get you the coverage you desire.

It is important that you spend some time researching your local media to observe the stories they tend to cover. By doing this, you'll be getting a general idea of what angle you can write your press release from to boost your chances of getting covered. It may also help to contact your local media and ask what kind of stories they are looking for. Try to avoid sounding like a press hog; just tell them that you thought the community would benefit by knowing about the various martial arts events in your area, and you wanted to know what they thought their readers/viewers/listeners would be interested in.

As for how to compose a press release, it should be written on a newsworthy topic. Write it like a news story, not like an ad for your school. Make sure to check it for spelling and grammar at least twice before you send it out; the last thing you want is to have a good story rejected for poor grammar. Also, it is extremely important that you write your press release from a factual and unbiased standpoint. Be objective when you write your story, and don't lie or stretch the truth. Any responsible journalist will tell you that a good news story is unbiased and sticks to the facts, so be honest and keep your opinions to yourself when writing your press release. And finally, make sure it's in a standard press release format (you can search the popular press release websites for sample press releases; just copy the format they use and you'll be fine).

Reporters can get very irritated when they find out that you have embellished the facts in order to increase your chances of making it to print. To drive home this point, I decided to ask a professional sports writer to explain this issue from his perspective. Olin Buchanan is a seasoned sports writer and family friend, and he was kind enough to share his insights on working with the press to get your story covered. I'd recommend that you pay close attention to what he has to say:

"In my experience the problem we've frequently faced with martial arts studios is often the facts have been misrepresented. For instance, we've been given results to a 'State championship' tournament only to learn that 'State tournament' actually consisted of about four studios — usually within 50 miles of each other — getting together for a tournament. Because that has happened so frequently, red flags go up immediately and editors feel the studios are just trying to get free advertising.

What I would suggest is that tournaments should include all the information. Where and when the tournament took place and who was involved (studios from different places and the age groups and skill levels involved). It would help to include a kid's career record... How many times he's won each match (not just tournaments). That way if he/she puts together a 50-0 record it might raise an editor's interest. Be as detailed as possible on who won or how they won.

Also, know your kid. If they have an interesting personal story — maybe he had to save up his own money to take lessons or perhaps he was tired of getting picked on in school or he has some kind of hardship that he/she is overcoming. But be TRUTHFUL because if there is some misinformation it's almost guaranteed that someone will call in. If misinformation is determined no newspaper will take the information again.

Further, I'd start at smaller, neighborhood newspapers first. Those papers are more geared toward community news, while a metro paper like Austin, Dallas, Fort Worth, San Antonio, etc., is going to focus on news that's going to be of interest to the masses — pro and college sports.

Now, if a student ends up in the Olympic Trials or something like that, of course, every newspaper would be interested in that."

Well, I believe that Olin's comments make it pretty clear; be factual and honest, and give details that are likely to perk the editor's interest. As he mentioned, if you can find a good human-interest angle, something that makes the story unique, that's all the better. Just make sure that you have your facts straight so you don't jeopardize your relationship with a particular writer or reporter at your local TV stations, radio stations or newspapers.

The Power of Networking

The idea of networking has become almost a cliché. However, the benefits of networking in your community for PR cannot be overestimated. Building a network of contacts that will spread the word about your school is like having money in the bank. Learn to network!

The Rules of Networking

Although various networking coaches and experts will use differing terminology to explain the following concepts, they are pretty much accepted by networking enthusiasts as being the core principles of the craft. Read and study them carefully, then apply them in your business life. If you do, you will reap the rewards of your efforts by attracting a steady stream of referrals to your business.

Rule #1: First, Be a Giver

Zig Ziglar is often quoted as saying, "You can have everything in life you want so long as you are willing to help enough other people get everything that they want." It is a brilliant philosophy and this quote epitomizes the mindset needed to become a successful networker. By giving to others first, you will create a reputation of being someone who helps get things done, thereby increasing your value to other people. Pretty soon, people will be knocking on your door wanting to get to know you; then you'll know you have done your job well.

Rule #2: Make a Habit of Building and Cultivating Relationships

Building and cultivating relationships is really what networking is all about. Making contacts is not enough; you have to build relationships with the people you contact so you can connect with them in a way that is mutually beneficial. Refer to rule #1 for guidance in fulfilling rule #2.

Rule #3: Keep Track of Your Contacts and Follow Up

You must be organized and keep track of your contacts. What good is it to meet someone who can assist you in meeting your goals, if you fail to get their contact information? You must keep track of the contacts you make so you can follow up on your initial contacts and fulfill the stated mission of rule #2.

Rule #4: Be Genuinely Interested in Other People

You will never be able to cultivate meaningful relationships with others until you learn to be genuinely interested in other people. This is one you just can't fake. If you have trouble with this, start by learning to have an open heart and by practicing at being a good listener. Just like I mentioned in the section on enrolling new students, listening is the first step to success in networking.

Rule #5: Seek Out Networking Opportunities and Attend Networking Events

It's a no-brainer, but it has to be mentioned. You must get out among other people, preferably in group situation to network. Even if you are shy and introverted, you must make yourself do this. Remember, you can't fish for trout in the middle of the Sahara – get out and go to places and events where you can meet new people!

Rule #6: Carry Your Business Cards and Hand Them Out Frequently

You want your contacts to be able to contact you as well, right? Okay then! Handing out your cards on a regular basis is the best way to get people to contact you when they desire your services. Carry your cards at all times and make it a habit to hand them out frequently.

Well, there you have it; six rules to assist you in becoming a networking success. They may sound simple, but don't let that fool you; following them to the "T" could make the difference between mediocrity and greatness for you and your business. If you doubt me, I challenge you to follow the Six Rules for six months, and see if I am mistaken. I'd bet a dollar to a donut that doing so will make a huge difference in your bottom line.

Effective Ad Design

I want to show you an example of an amateurish ad; in fact, it's the first ad I ever ran for my business. Interestingly enough, the ad worked, despite its poor design; little did I know that the ad integrated some of the key features that are crucial to good ad design.

But, I was lucky – and as I later discovered, you need more than luck to succeed in today's economy. Let's critique it and use it as an example of how you should go about designing a good ad.

As you can see, the ad design is a very simple, no frills print ad. Now, as far as good ad design goes, every ad needs to be designed around four elements in order to be effective. The use of these four elements in advertising is called the AIDA Principle. These elements are:

1. **Attention**: Every ad needs an attention-getter to attract the reader's eye. In this ad, I used a simple silhouette of my instructor delivering a flying side kick. These days I would pay for a nice looking photo from a stock photography website. (And yes, I drew that picture.)

2. **Interest**: An ad needs to gain the reader's interest as well. The heading, "Karate Classes," was displayed prominently in the ad in an attempt to gain the reader's

interest. Not the best headline, to be sure. In fact, a good headline needs to both capture attention, and make a powerful promise to the reader. It should also compel them to read the rest of the ad. Not a total fail here, but not great, either.

3. **Desire**: Okay, here's where this ad really failed. I didn't do anything to create desire in the reader to take my classes. In every good ad, there should always be strong ad copy (that's marketing-speak for text) that explains exactly why the product or service being presented in an ad is beneficial to the consumer.

4. **Action**: This ad has a weak call to action. Every good ad must have a strong call to action; something that creates within the reader a desire to respond to the ad immediately. What I might have done is offer a free uniform or an introductory discount as a limited-time offer, a technique that is commonly used as a call to action in martial arts ads today.

As I said, despite my hit-or-miss approach to my initial marketing, I did manage to get a decent response from this ad. Other reasons why this ad worked had to do with the fact it is relatively clean and uncluttered, which makes it easy to read. Also, I unwittingly made effective use of "white space" in the ad, which tends to draw the reader's attention and helps to keep them in the ad. It was also short and sweet, which gets the reader to the end of the ad quickly. Using minimal ad copy is not always the best tact for an ad, but in situations where you are competing with many other ads or where the reader might not have time to read a lot of copy, it is the way to go. So, I got lucky and made good with this ad.

Other negative aspects of this ad are its amateurish look and the extensive use of difficult to read fonts. Fonts such as Arial and Franklin Gothic are often easier to read than Times New Roman because they are sans-serif fonts; they don't have all those extra curlycues that make them harder to make out in an ad or sign. As for the design, fortunately the paper that this ad ran in was small and local; my ad was probably one of the more professional looking ads that ran in it. However, in a larger paper my ad would have stood out like a sore thumb; that's the kind of attention that you do not want for your ad.

So, you should now have a basic idea of what elements should go into an ad. A good ad needs an attention-getter, it needs to quickly create interest with its design or headline, it needs to have good ad copy to create a desire for your product or service, and it needs a strong call to action to increase the response.

Now, let's examine a more recent ad I created, and critique it using the A-I-D-A Principle as a guideline:

1. **Attention**: For an attention getter I chose a picture that I found on a stock photo site. I think this picture does a good job of attracting attention. The fact that I used the picture in this ad shows that you don't necessarily need to hire a photographer to come in and take pictures of your students for every ad you run. Another technique that I used here was to use a dotted border around the coupon. Some might consider this to be an example of poor graphic design; however, it is an easy and effective way to draw attention to your ad.

2. **Interest**: I attempted to build interest in the ad by using a strong headline to increase the reader's curiosity. When the reader sees the headline, they should be thinking, "I

can identify with that – this sounds like my kind of workout!" Even with consumers being as skeptical as they are today, you can still get their attention by creating a connection with them in your headline.

3. **Desire**: This ad is geared toward adults that might want to get back into shape after the holidays. It would normally be run in January and February as a seasonal promotion. Therefore, the ad copy speaks directly to the target market and their desire to get fit; but it also addresses two of the main problems most adults have with sticking to an exercise program; quick results and boredom (they are learning a skill as they get in shape). By addressing those issues in the copy, the ad attempts to build perceived value in the reader's mind.

4. **Action**: The call to action is expressed and driven home with an expiration date on the "special offer" coupon. An even stronger call to action is to give away classes for free, maybe a week or even a month, but only for a limited time and only for a limited number of people – for example, *"the first ten people who sign up on our website get their first month free"*. Just make sure you stick to your ad offer... in other words, once you get your ten people to respond, you need to take that registration form off your website. Speaking of which, *I forgot to include my website address in this ad – big mistake!* Be sure to include your web address in everything you put out.

One additional and very important element in this ad is the inclusion of my company name in bold letters. This helps to build **brand awareness** and to get the consumer to associate martial arts instruction with my company. You could also include your logo if you have space in the ad. If a logo is designed well and it sticks out in the reader's mind, they will recognize it the next time they see your ad and associate "martial arts" with your school. This is why you should take time designing your logo; you want something that stands out among your competition. Remember, generic logos won't help you at all in improving your overall ad response rates. Pick a logo that leaves a strong impression in the consumer's mind, one that includes your name and a simple graphic.

Well, I certainly hope that this chapter helped you understand the basic aspects of effective marketing. I know that I spent more time writing this chapter than any other in the manual; however, I felt like this chapter deserved the time I gave it, simply because the skills I covered here are some of the most important that you will learn in your quest to be a "Small Dojo Big Profits" success story. If you will just study this chapter again and again, and follow the advice I gave you here faithfully, you will always have a steady stream of students knocking on your dojo door.

Now, let's get on with the next chapter concerning the flip side of marketing and advertising: Retention!

ELEVEN

NOW THAT YOU HAVE THEM, HOW WILL YOU KEEP THEM?

Strategies for Increased Student Retention

In the previous chapter we discussed how to attract students. Now, we need to spend some time discussing how you are going to retain those students for the long haul, so they keep paying their tuition month-after-month and year-after-year. Retention is one of the most overlooked and undervalued aspects of martial arts business management; yet, it is probably the one problem area that will keep most new martial arts school owners from achieving great financial success.

I will readily admit that this is an area in which I have fallen short in the past; there was a time when I felt that I could afford to be lazy when it came to retention, since I never had a hard time attracting new students and I really never cared for the idea of managing a large student enrollment. This was a foolish mistake on my part; if people are leaving your school, it is wise to learn the reasons why they are leaving. If I had taken the time to work on my student retention, I could have avoided losing some of my staunchest supporters and clients.

Reasons Why Students Drop Out

Each and every martial arts student that begins taking martial arts classes has dreams and goals. For some, it is achieving Black Belt; for others, it is to gain self-confidence; and for others still, it may be to get in shape; the list could go on and on. Sadly, most people that begin training in the martial arts never make it to black belt; moreover, many never even stick around long enough to make it past the beginner level! As instructors and school owners, we must examine the reasons for this. Some of the most reliable industry information we have on student attrition shows that:

- The number one reason that students drop out is because they develop a perception that the instructor is indifferent to their progress; in other words, something happens that makes them feel like their instructor doesn't care.
- The second most common reason students drop out is boredom.
- Getting injured or the fear of getting injured is another big reason why students drop out. For many, they will develop this fear around the same time that they start sparring.
- Students that feel they have been insulted or humiliated will be gone before you can say "adios."
- If a student or parent feels that the benefits of studying the martial arts are not worth the cost, they will drop out.
- If a student loses respect for their instructor(s), they will drop out.
- About 3-7% of students will quit taking classes for reasons beyond our control. This is due to time and work constraints, or they have to move away due to a job transfer, and so forth. These types of unpreventable

dropouts are due to what I call insensible student attrition.

I would like to point out to you that, with the exception of insensible student attrition, in each one of these situations the instructor is able to take measures beforehand to prevent the student from dropping out. While in certain rare instances a family will go through a catastrophic event that seriously effects their finances (death of spouse/parent, lay-off/loss of job, or long-term illness), in most cases when a client comes to you stating that they are having difficulty paying their tuition what they are really telling you is that they don't see any benefit in spending their disposable income on your classes anymore.

Case In Point:

In the earlier days of running my studio, I had the time to make myself available to my clients in the daytime hours when I wasn't teaching classes. Years later, when I reentered college, I wasn't able to spend as much time at the studio outside of our regular class schedule.

By suddenly limiting my availability to my clients, I was unwittingly alienating them. They had come to expect that I would be accessible during the daytime to answer their questions and hear their concerns, and did not like the fact that I was no longer available all the time. From my perspective I was still teaching good classes like I always had, so I couldn't see what the big deal was. To my students, however, it appeared as though I no longer cared about them. I soon started to lose longtime students over this seemingly inconsequential issue.

The moral here is simply this; you must keep close tabs on the issues that cause dissention among your clientele. While from your perspective you may be doing everything right, your clients might have a completely different take on the events at hand. Not paying attention to what the majority of your clients want will eventually end up costing you students and money.

As I said earlier, this usually has to do with a belief that the instructor does not care about their progress (or lack thereof), or boredom, or both. If the instructor is teaching great classes and takes the time to show a personal interest in each and every student (which is a constant challenge, but a worthwhile pursuit nonetheless), these situations will rarely come up. Accordingly the best methods to prevent drop outs are to get to know your students and to teach exciting classes.

But what about when a client doesn't think that martial arts lessons are worth the expense anymore? Think about it; if a client is initially excited enough to make a one-, two-, or three-year commitment to train in the martial arts, then they suddenly lose interest, something must have happened to cause them to want to quit. There are usually only two possibilities as to why this would happen; either the instructor hasn't been doing a good job in demonstrating the benefits to the client, or the school has slipped up on a client service issue. And, often as not, it is a customer service issue that is the culprit in these situations.

Retaining Perceived Value with the Consumer: Consistency is Key

Retaining perceived value means that your clients continue to believe that they are getting their money's worth at your studio. This is perhaps the most important way to improve your retention and increase your renewals. But, what does it take to accomplish this?

First, let's look at what it takes to establish value in the client's eyes:

- When you enroll a new student, you naturally want to create this perception of value by promising to assist them in solving their problems and meeting their goals through martial arts training.
- You also must teach an exciting introductory course, and you have to teach awesome, high-energy, motivating classes every single day.
- Additionally, you must go beyond just teaching technique by delving into the philosophies and mental training that make the martial arts a valuable tool for building character.
- In short, you must exceed the client's expectations.

Now, let's take a look at the situation I described above. In my case, I had developed a great rapport and a lot of loyalty with my clientele by offering a level of service that the other schools in my area didn't offer. I didn't think anything of it at the time, but for my clients the personal touch I offered by personally taking their calls every day really meant a lot to them. In retrospect, I was probably guilty of spoiling my clients; nevertheless, I should not have given them such a high level of service if I wasn't willing to continue to offer the same great level of service on a long-term basis.

One of the first things you should do before you ever open your doors is to define the parameters of the quality of service that you are willing to provide to your customers. Are you going to be open every day from 9 AM to 9 PM or from 1 PM to 9 PM? Will you personally take all the calls when you are at the studio, or will you hire an answering service or office manager to do it for you? Will you have an open door policy, or will you see your clients on an appointment-only basis? You should give these sorts of issues a great deal of thought, because in later years your customers will define the perceived value of the service they continue to receive based on the initial level of service you provided them when they first enrolled.

Once you define these parameters, you must not deviate from

your established level of service, unless you do so by exceeding the standards of service you have provided in the past. For instance, if you have always allowed your current students to attend unlimited classes, you cannot suddenly limit their attendance to only two classes per week. That doesn't mean that you can't place such limits on new memberships; it just means that it would be unfair to take those privileges away from your existing clientele without giving something back to them in return.

Always keep in mind that maintaining consistency in your quality of service is crucial to retaining your clients for the long haul. If there is one thing that will spell certain death for your business, it is being inconsistent in the quality of service that you provide your clients. Now that you understand this, let's move on and discuss the specific tasks that you must accomplish on a regular basis to keep your retention high and your dropout rate as low as possible.

Plugging the Holes in Your Retention

Now I am going to get into the nuts and bolts of plugging the holes in your retention. There are three specific goals that you must meet on a regular basis to keep your retention high:

- You have to ensure that your students are in fact making good progress in their training -
- You have to make your students aware that they are making progress -
- And, you have to let your students know that you care about whether or not they are making progress.

Let's examine how you can specifically go about accomplishing each of these tasks.

Ensuring and Demonstrating Student Progress, Showing That You Care

The most common method for showing students that they are progressing is through belt rank exams. However, belt rank exams can be stressful and intimidating, and therefore counter-productive to a student's progress. Of course, this is a catch-22; if the tests are too easy, they aren't a good measure of the student's progress, but if they are too hard, students will be tempted to drop out to avoid running the risk of failure on an exam. So, what is an instructor to do? Well, here are some suggestions to make things go a little smoother on exam days:

- **Hold monthly progress checks in class.** This is a long-standing tradition in most modern schools. Holding an informal "mock exam" each month can help you identify problem areas before they get out of hand, and it can assist your students in performing better by allowing them to get additional feedback regarding the expected performance on their next exam. It may also be helpful to give out belt stripes to students who reach certain preset performance standards on each progress check.

- **Use a progressive system of performance expectations.** This simply means that you take it a little easier on new students, easing them into the routine. All beginners should have at least a three-month adjustment period before they are expected to understand etiquette and courtesy in the studio. Physical performance requirements should also be progressive; in other words, expect beginners to perform like beginners, intermediate students to perform like intermediate students, and advanced students to perform like advanced students. Don't expect a yellow belt to perform like a black belt.

- **Design your curriculum so the belt ranks (or stages of advancement, if you don't use belts) are attainable for the average person.** I know the old philosophy quite well; "If it is easy to get, it isn't worth having in the first place." While this is true to an extent, it is also true that no one will stay at your school if your curriculum is impossible to progress through. I recommend that you break your curriculum down so that your first year progression is very light, maybe just enough to introduce a student to the basics. Then, in the second and third years you can gradually start increasing the amount of material a student must know at each rank. Be careful that you don't make your curriculum too "top-heavy"; that is, don't leave the bulk of the material at the brown belt ranks. Spread it out a little so each rank is progressively more challenging but not so that it is insurmountable to learn all the requirements for an advanced rank.

Of course, there are other ways to show your students that they are making progress besides awarding them with rank.

- **Videotaping your students.** One school I know of videotapes each student during their first lesson, then at six months, one year, 18 months, and so on. They then review the student's tapes at every renewal conference to effectively illustrate the progress that each student has made. From a practical perspective, this is a great way to prove that you have done an adequate job as an instructor.
- **Using merit badges and stars.** I also know of several studios that use merit badges, star patches, and

other reward systems. Much like the merit badges that are used in scouting, students are given specific performance tasks that they must accomplish before they can receive a merit badge or star. Once they demonstrate the requisite skills and knowledge, they are allowed to wear the badge on their uniform. If you style or system does not allow for extraneous decorations on the gi or dobak, merit badges may be substituted with certificates of achievement.

- **Sending out Good Job Notes.** One of the simplest and most personal methods of letting your students know that they are progressing is to send out Good Job Notes. This entails sitting down for ten minutes a day and writing out good job notes to five or ten students chosen from your current enrollment. It is best to go through your student roster alphabetically by class, with a goal of sending a note out to each student at least once a month. These notes should be hand-written and should include an original and personal message for each and every student. It is okay to use mailing labels, but it looks better when they are addressed by hand.
- **Stickers**. Lastly, for young children, you can hand out stickers at the end of every class as a reward for good behavior and effort. I used to do this in every Little Dragons class, and the kids really worked hard for their daily sticker. If one of them got out of hand, I would give them two warnings; on the third transgression, I would withhold their sticker. This worked wonders for behavior in the 4-6 year old group.

Tracking Attendance

In order to increase your retention, you will have to track your attendance. It is a well-known fact that students who start missing classes on a regular basis will soon drop out completely. Tracking attendance allows you to catch the students who miss classes so you can discover why they are not attending class. Then, you may address their situation individually to encourage them to return to class and to improve their level of enthusiasm and quality of attendance.

Tracking attendance used to be a real pain. But, with the advent of modern technology, it is now a very simple task to do. All it takes is a good software program and a decent barcode scanner or hot key reader, and you can have students check in automatically at the front counter at every class.

I recommend that you examine your attendance statistics every Wednesday and Friday morning. That way, you can see who missed class the first two days of the week, and give them an MIA ("missing in action") phone call to let them know that they were missed and to find out if they are doing okay. On Friday morning, you will want to send out MIA notes to any student that missed class during that week; this is nothing more than a note or post card that says, "Hey, we noticed your absence and we look forward to seeing you in class soon." Incidentally, doing this by email or text is fine, but I prefer a written note as I think it means more to the client. This individual attention does take a little more effort than just leaving the students to their own designs, but it will go a long way toward bringing your retention to an acceptable level.

Sometimes, They Just Slip Through...

According to industry statistics, every month you will lose between 3% and 7% of your total enrollment to insensible student attrition, and there is basically nothing you can do about it. People will drop out for reasons that are totally beyond your control; they get sick, they move away, they get married and have babies, or for various other reasons no longer have the time to attend class. What this means is that no matter how good your customer service is, you will lose a small chunk of your roster every single month.

So, should you even be worried about attrition if students are going to leave anyway? Isn't it just easier to concentrate on marketing and just keep a steady flow of new students rolling in? The answers to the preceding questions are "Absolutely!" and "Absolutely not!" Knowing what we know about attrition, you must become very good at keeping your students motivated as well as consistently working very hard to attract new students.

Numbers-wise, think about it like this:

- If you have an enrollment of 180 active students, and you lose 5% of those students every month, if you never recruited another student again you would lose nearly every single student you have within 20 months. Pretty scary, right?
- But, if you attract nine new students per month, at the end of that same twenty-month period your school would have grown to 190 students, provided that your attrition rate remained constant during the same period.
- Now, if you reduce your attrition rate to just 3%, and attract just 8 new students per month, your enrollment will increase to over 230 students.

Do you see how minute improvements in your dropout rate can have a serious impact on your overall numbers? For more on this topic, be sure to read my book titled *The Profit-Boosting Principles: How to Dramatically Increase Your Martial Arts School Profits Without Increasing Your Overhead*, available through Amazon.com. Also, check out the section on benchmarks in the Appendix.

Success Strategy: The bottom line is that the more effective you are at increasing your new enrollments and decreasing your attrition rate, the bigger your total student enrollment will become.

How to Teach So Your Students Stick Around

In case I failed to make this clear in previous sections of this book, let me state it plainly for you here and now:

> ***Key Concept:*** *You must offer quality martial arts instruction and teach exciting, high-energy classes in order to retain students for the long haul.*

You may be asking yourself, "If this is so important, why did he wait so long to cover it?" Well, quite frankly it's because I know that most martial arts instructors tend to gloss over business management issues, instead focusing almost entirely on curriculum and training in their studios. That's why so many martial arts school owners struggle – they ignore the business basics. If I covered teaching and curriculum earlier in the manual, you probably would have read that chapter, skimmed through the rest of the book, only to run out and fail miserably at starting a studio (deny it all you want, but I'm a dyed-in-the-wool martial arts enthusiast myself; I know how it you tick).

For some of you, right now you are thinking that you already know all there is to know about teaching good martial arts classes. Think again! While you may be an expert in the technical aspects of your system, that doesn't necessarily mean that you can convey that information effectively in your classes, not to mention doing it in a manner that is both engaging and entertaining.

Yes, that's right; I said the "E" word: entertaining. You may as well come to grips with it right now, because a big part of your job from here on out is keeping your clients entertained. That doesn't mean that you have to take acting lessons (although taking a public speaking class wouldn't hurt) or that you have to start cracking jokes and being silly in all your classes; it simply means that you have to work at teaching classes that are fresh and exciting every single day.

Another issue is how to teach your students without destroying their confidence. We are supposed to be building others up, not tearing them down, remember? Doing the old "Full Metal Jacket" drill instructor routine is not going to make you a better instructor; all it will accomplish is to chase your students out the door in quick order.

For you die-hards that get all misty-eyed when you think back to the good old days when your instructor berated and belittled you and how it made you a better black belt, I want you to consider how many students your abusive instructor had in their studio; I would hazard a guess and say that it was not too many. I am sure that their retention was dismal and that the only people who stayed around long enough to earn an advanced rank were the people who didn't really need any help in the areas of fitness, confidence, or self-defense skills anyway.

While I am on the topic, here's a little history lesson for you to put things in perspective:

- The first Americans to bring back the martial arts from Asia were mostly soldiers who had been stationed in Japan and Korea, to help rebuild those countries after we helped tear them up in World War II and the Korean War.
- Common sense and historical accounts will tell you that most Asians resented the occupation, disliked us "round-eyes," and weren't too keen on sharing their cultural heritage with Westerners. However, American money was always in demand, and GI's tend to spend it fast, so despite their overall attitude of resentment they taught us *gaijin* anyway.
- However, they were under no obligation to be nice about it. American soldiers and other Westerners were subjected to some of the most brutal training they had

ever experienced, and it wasn't necessarily always part of the regular program. They were routinely treated worse than the Asian students, and prejudice ran rampant in the dojo and dojang where they trained.

- Combine all these factors with the fact that these guys were soldiers who were accustomed to using strong and sometimes cruel disciplinary tactics in the course of their work, and what do you get? An entire generation of really tough martial arts instructors that had mean streaks a mile wide.

- Consequently, when they returned to the States, it was only natural that they should pass it on to their students.

Now, the question is, when do we break the cycle? If you want to be successful in your martial arts studio, right now would be a good time. You have to learn to accept the fact that your American students are generally not going to be too keen on taking the same type of treatment that you may have received from your instructor. Now, that doesn't mean that you aren't going to have discipline and respect in your studio; it only means that you must find other ways of instilling it.

Updating Your Teaching Methods

Modern teaching methods in the martial arts were pioneered by some of the more successful school owners way before I came along. While I didn't invent any of the following strategies, I am going to list and explain some of the techniques that they implemented in their programs that have worked well for me in my studio over the years. I strongly suggest that you start using these methods in your classes to increase your retention and more effectively motivate your students.

1. **Praise-Correct-Praise (PCP).** This one is an old standby that isn't really discussed much nowadays, probably because it's been

taken for granted that everyone knows it. PCP involves being a "good finder," always finding something positive about what the student is doing. Specifically, you start by first pointing out a positive and desired behavior a student is exhibiting; next giving correction where needed; and then ending the interaction with more praise. For example: "Great front stance, Jimmy, I like the way you are bending that knee – nice and deep! Now, let's just chamber that fist a little higher, above the belt. That's it, excellent! That's the way a Black Belt does it!" *It is important when using PCP that the praise you give is genuine,* that you only correct one major error in each interaction, and that you always end the interaction on a high note.

2. **Positive Reframing.** Positive reframing is simply avoiding the use of negatives when giving instructions. For instance, if you want a class to kick higher, instead of stating, "I don't want to see anyone kicking below their belts" you would say, "Okay everyone, I want to see every kick go as high as you can get it!" Positively worded phrases send the proper message to the student, which is that we want them to succeed, and we are here to help them do so. Negative phrases will make the student feel as if they are failing, so always use Positive Reframing when giving instruction or directions.

3. **Tell-Show-Do.** Tell-Show-Do is a way of integrating all five major learning styles (structured, sociological, auditory, visual, and tactile) into every class. In Tell-Show-Do, you first use a spoken instructional sequence for the auditory learners, and then you demonstrate the movement for the visual learners, followed by solo practice for the tactile learners, and finally integrating group and partnered practice for structured and sociological learners. In this manner, you are addressing individuality in learning styles and making sure that each and every student is able to absorb the information and curriculum.

4. **Disguising Repetition**. I like to say that repetition is the mother of all skill, but it is also the father of boredom and dropouts. Disguising repetition is perhaps the most important thing you can do to keep your classes interesting and engaging. When it comes to

disguising repetition, I only have two words for you: Be creative! Try to change the way you teach a skill every time you teach it, especially after the students have the acquired the basics of a particular movement or technique. Examples of ways to disguise repetition are:

- Using combinations
- Adding jumping and spinning to a move
- Using props (pads, bags, and targets)
- Balancing on one foot
- Multiple target combos (multiple props)
- Jumping over an obstacle before, during, or after performing a technique
- Partner drills and practice
- Blindfolded training
- Doing moves in reverse order

5. **Vocalization and Engagement.** You must speak clearly and project your voice to everyone in the room. It is important that you find your "command voice." The command voice is not yelling, but a projected speaking voice that reaches all corners of the teaching area. Some mistakes to avoid are:

- **Talking at the wall or away from the students**. Always face the students or turn your head toward them when giving commands.
- **Talking at the floor**. Keep your head level when addressing the class.
- **Not making eye contact**. You should frequently make eye contact with your students when teaching class.
- **Teaching to the center or the front of the room only**. You should walk around and circulate to every area of the room. And that leads me to the next teaching technique...

6. **Walking the Lines.** Walking the lines is a great way to ensure that you make individual contact with every single student in every single class. This personal attention will go a long way toward showing your students that you care. Your goal is to engage each student with eye contact and PCP at least three times in every single class. To do this, you have to walk the lines at least once every fifteen minutes or so. Spend no more than 15-30 seconds with each student, use PCP, and end each contact and interaction on a high note.

7. **No Downtime.** No downtime means that you keep the class moving at all times, never letting the action stop. For adults, this is usually pretty easy, but with kids it can be a challenge. Some suggestions:

- **Brevity.** Make your explanations as short and concise as possible. Avoid giving long-winded explanations of technique.
- **Variety.** Change things up a lot. For adults and teens, change the pace every five minutes or so. For kids 7-12, change things up about every three minutes. For age 6 and under, change things every 1-2 minutes (yes, you will be worn out after your kid's classes).
- **Timing.** Save verbal history lessons for break time; Q & A sessions and mat chats (pep talks that cover philosophy and character building concepts) should be saved for the end of each class.

8. **Use A Written Lesson Plan For Every Single Class.**
Don't even think about stepping out on the floor without a written lesson plan. Lesson plans keep you on track and they help you ensure that you are covering the necessary curriculum for any upcoming exams. Type up your lesson plans for each class and rank level and save them in a single document. Then at the end of the year, you'll never have to write another one again.

Renewals

Getting renewals should come relatively easy if you are doing all of the things I listed previously in this chapter. Even so, here are a few tips to assist you in getting the majority of your students to renew:

- Schedule renewal conferences at least 30 days in advance so you'll have time to address any concerns that your clients may have with their training.
- Send out renewal reminders to all your students who are coming up for renewal at least 60 days in advance. This will help you to avoid springing it on them at the last moment, and it allows them to budget for any additional renewal fees they might have to pay.
- Including an automatic renewal option on your membership agreements is a great idea. If you are allowed by law to do this in your state, by all means do so.
- Encourage your students to renew early and often by offering money-saving incentives for early renewal. You might waive their yearly membership fee if they renew more than 30 days in advance, or let them continue to pay the same tuition rates if they continue their membership in an uninterrupted fashion for another year or two, regardless of what you are currently charging your new students. Advertise these specials to your students so they know to take advantage of them.

One More Strategy You Might Not Have Considered...

There is one strategy for improving retention that some people never even think about. What is it? Make your studio a social center for your students. This means that you have special events every month. I suggest that you host parties for your students that are free of charge around the holidays, when school lets out, in mid-summer, and when school starts in the fall. You might also sponsor "field trips" to seminars and tournaments, host special events for your Leadership Team, and have Customer Appreciation Days where you have refreshments for all your customers. Be creative in giving your clients the opportunity to mingle and get to know you, your staff, and each other. By doing so you will be creating close bonds that encourage loyalty and commitment to the studio, and your renewals and retentions will reflect this accordingly.

That should be enough information to help you keep your retention and renewal rates high and your attrition low. Take this aspect of school management seriously! Attrition can be a real profit-killer, so keep an eye on your attendance, and stay on top of your renewals.

Now, on to one of my favorite martial arts school management topics: multiple profit centers!

TWELVE
MULTIPLE PROFIT CENTERS

Or, Paying the Light Bill When Things Are Tight

When the economy went sour right after the September 11th attacks, we experienced one of the worst back-to-school enrollment seasons ever. Since my school was located in a town that employs a lot of people in the high-tech sector, we lost about a third of our clients to lay-offs and transfers, and our new enrollments were dismal, to say the least. My numbers were slipping, it was coming up on the holiday season, and I was facing the prospect of having to lay-off all of my employees, something that I just couldn't do, especially not right before the holidays. I had to do something quick to increase my revenues!

Thankfully, I had spent a considerable amount of time and effort learning about multiple profit centers (MPCs). MPCs (sometimes called "added profit centers") are methods you can use to create additional income streams in your business. The most obvious MPC to implement and the one that usually creates the greatest additional income for most schools during the holidays is the Pro Shop. Knowing this, I was quickly able to generate several thousand dollars of additional revenue by holding an inventory clearance sale and clearing out much of my slow-moving and over-stocked inventory. To make a short story shorter, Christmas was saved (*sigh*).

Not only can MPCs help you pull through when you are in a tight spot financially, they can also help you increase your profits and earn you a considerable amount of additional income on a year-round basis. Your Pro Shop alone should be good for getting an additional $5-10 per month in **profit** from each student on your roster. That should amount to an additional $1,000 to $2,000 in profit per month for a good-sized "Small Dojo Big Profits" studio.

And, that's just the tip of the iceberg. The following is a rundown of several different MPCs you can use in your studio and the potential for profit that each MPC has.

A Break Down of MPCs

The Pro Shop- Like I said, your Pro Shop should be good for an additional profit of about $5-$10 per student per month. Keys to having a successful Pro Shop are:

- Locate the Pro Shop on the right side of your studio as you enter the front door. Marketing studies have shown that people will most often glance to their right when entering a room, so this is the best place to put your Pro Shop for maximum exposure.
- Purchase at least one glass display case and use "slat board" on the walls of the Pro Shop so you can keep your most popular items and seasonal items in plain view. A good place to get this stuff cheap is to scope out department stores that are going out of business; approach the management and ask them if they are selling any of their fixtures. They'll usually let a few pieces go for pennies on the dollar.
- Study the merchandize displays at your local department

stores. Model your displays on the methods they use. Note that bright colors and seasonal tie-ins help to attract the customer's eye.

- Avoid price competition. Only carry equipment that can't be found in the big sporting goods stores, or "private label" your school's sparring gear and uniforms so the students are compelled to purchase them in your studio. Failing this, try to find a supplier that sells easy-to-find items, like sparring gear and student uniforms, at a much lower wholesale rate so you can at least match the sporting goods store prices.

- Offer convenience. Post your Pro Shop hours and offer equipment ordering 24/7 on your website. Century has a really cool program going right now for about $40 per month that allows you to get a great looking merchant website selling their products. For what you'll save in shipping, it'll pay for itself – I recommend that you get one ASAP.

- Accept credit cards. Accepting credit cards will increase your sales (and your tuition cash outs). You can even lease a credit card terminal if you don't want to buy one outright (but I suggest buying one wholesale as it's much cheaper). You can also purchase point of sale software and a credit card scanner and use your front desk computer to swipe credit cards for Pro Shop sales. It doesn't matter how you do it, just do it.

- Change your display and rotate your merchandise every month. Eliminating the possibility that your clients will get tired of seeing the same old displays all the time will keep clients interested in your Pro Shop year round.

- Be certain that the price of every item is clearly marked, and use "even-odd" pricing (prices ending in "7's" and "9's") on every product. Examples: "$9.99" instead of "$10".

- Make sure that you make at least a 50% profit margin on every item you sell. Simply double the wholesale cost of the product, add 5% for shipping, and you'll be in the ballpark of 50% profit. Example: A uniform wholesales for $12 and you sell it for $24.99.

Belt Exam Fees and Graduation Nights- Belt exam fees are a sometimes controversial topic, but they are a good source of additional income for a martial arts school owner. I don't see anything wrong with charging a fee that covers certification, exams, and graduation ceremonies; universities and government licensing boards do it all the time. Just don't gouge your students - schools that charge as much in testing fees as they do in tuition are just plain dishonest in my opinion. Also, make sure that you are giving value in exchange for the fee. Hosting a nice graduation ceremony after every exam is a good way to do this and it does wonders for retention. If you charge $25 per exam (a very reasonable rate) and you have 200 students testing quarterly, you should be making about $1,500+ per month on testing fees.

Vending Machines- They don't pay for themselves very quickly, and can be a hassle to stock and clean. However, if you can get some vending machines secondhand at an auction or pawn shop, I highly recommend it. You can buy candy and drinks in bulk at Sam's or Costco, and you should be able to make about a 50-75% profit margin on what you sell. But, don't use an outside vending company! You won't make anything off them, and you might end up having to stock the machines yourself to boot. If you sell 50 drinks and 50 snacks a week (easy to do) at $1.00 each, profiting .60 cents per, you should be profiting about $250.00 per month off your vending sales.

Special Events- Hosting special events at your studio should allow you to bring in about an additional $25-$30 per student every three months or so. Don't expect every student to attend every special event you hold, however. A good estimate would be that an involved student will attend about four special events per year. As a rule of thumb, a 200-student school should be making in the range of $1,000 to $1,500 on special events every month. Some profitable special events that you can host are:

- **Seminars:** Teaching seminars on special topics is a good way to earn extra cash at your dojo. It is best to teach a kid's seminar one month, one for the teens the next month, and an adult seminar the third month, then cycle back through. Spreading them out like that will ensure higher attendance at each event. Seminar topics could include weapons, grappling, street self-defense, rape prevention (get some training here; I've been certified to teach women's self-defense for years, and the stuff I've seen some instructors teaching is enough to make my head spin, it's so bad), or winning tournament sparring techniques; the possibilities are endless. One word of advice; don't bring in an "expert" unless you think you can attract enough people to cover his or her fees and expenses. I've taken a wash on hosting "big names" before, and it's not a pleasant experience.

- **Parent's Night Out (PNO):** This is a special event for kids ages 5-12 that allows their parents to get out of the house without having to worry about who is watching their kids. We usually charge about $25.00-$30.00 for a four hour PNO, which consists of a karate class, group games, video games, snacks & pizza, and a movie when the kids are winding down. Make sure that each kid signs in, and get a release form signed by the parent of any child who isn't a member of your school. Try to have a 10-to-1 child to adult ratio, and keep things moving to avoid any rowdiness. Clearly post the pick-up times; you might even want to assess stiff late fees to any parents that pick their child up late without calling or without a good reason.

- **Laser Tag Night:** Go to Toys-R-Us and buy five sets of Laser Challenge guns and vests (it'll cost about $100 for 10 guns and vests). Then, host a "Laser Challenge Night!" where you decorate the school in neon and glow-in-the-dark colors, maybe using black lights or strobe lights, with bags and mats set up so the kids can hide behind them (be sure to cover your mirrors with Kraft paper or else the reflected laser beams will ruin your evening). Charge about $20 a head for a two-hour party, and include some inexpensive drinks for the kids in the price. One warning: this event takes a lot of careful planning and supervision! Use some common sense in your set up, and make the kids take turns playing in small groups that you rotate through every five or ten minutes. Also, have some video game consoles set up around the school so the kids have something to do when they are not playing laser tag.
- **School Tournaments:** Another great event that is always a winner. Order some martial arts medals from a wholesale supplier (I get them at a lower price by going directly to the trophy manufacturer). I suggest that you have medals for 1st – 4th place, and ribbons for all participants. Charge about $10 per participant for one event, $5 per additional event. Events might include forms, sparring, weapons, self-defense, and breaking. Make a big show of handing out the awards, and take lots of pictures.

Private Lessons- I know of studios that cater to the adult market in which their entire business model is based on offering private lessons, much like a golf-instruction or flying instruction business. Personally, I don't care to teach privates, but that's just my own personal preference; otherwise, I think it's a strong business model. However, if you are just going to teach private lessons on the side, you should charge a minimum of 50% of your base monthly tuition per hour for private lessons. Give a 10% discount for advance payment when lessons are purchased in blocks of ten, and a 40% discount for individuals who partner up to take lessons together (schedule no more than three at a time, just to keep the quality high). If you get just two clients taking a single one-hour private lesson per week, that's an additional $400+ per month in your pocket. Not too shabby for eight hours of your time. Also, if you are fitness-oriented and like to work out, you can get certified as a personal trainer and offer fitness training on the side for similar rates.

Teaching At Another Location- As I stated earlier, when I first got started I taught at many different locations outside of my studio in order to make ends meet. Universities, colleges, daycares, elementary and middle schools, after school programs, recreation and community centers; these are all good places to teach part-time to make some extra money and contacts, and I have had programs of some form at every one. For example, I made roughly $500 a month working three hours a week teaching a class for the kinesiology department at the local university. While it wasn't a huge amount of money, it helped out quite a bit during the early period when I was just starting my business.

Bringing In Outside Instructors- No, not martial arts instructors; I've tried that and it never works. What I am suggesting is to bring in instructors that can teach programs that are totally unrelated to what you do. Pilates, yoga, tai chi, and aerobics classes are some suggestions. These programs tend to be a good way to utilize your space and make some additional cash during the early morning hours when you aren't using your studio. You can opt to pay the instructor directly and take on all the responsibility of collecting payments, advertisement and marketing (you'll make more money) or you can work on a split for a fraction of what the instructor makes. Either way, it makes good sense to do; a three-day per week class with only ten students can bring in $1,200 a month gross.

Summer   Camps   and   After-School   Pick-up

Programs- I know that a lot of people in the industry sing the praises of after-school karate programs and summer camps, but they aren't telling the whole story. I have just a few words to offer in describing my experiences with running summer camps and after-school pick-up programs: good money, big headaches. In a nutshell, they do make a lot of money but I personally don't care for all the extra responsibility involved.

Essentially, if you decide to run after-school and summer camps you'll be operating a daycare facility. Because of this, there are things that you must know in order to stay out of trouble with the authorities and with the parents of the children who will attend your programs. For example, I personally know of martial arts instructors who have lost their schools because they got shut down by their state daycare licensing agency for running unlicensed daycare centers out of their studios.

I also know of instructors who were wrongly accused of abusing the children in their program. Even thought they were cleared of all wrongdoing, the damage to their reputation was immense; it is not something that you will easily bounce back from should it happen to you.

Aside from the potential legal pitfalls surrounding camp programs, there are more mundane negatives that are worth mentioning. For one, the difference between having a student at your school for two hours a week and having that student for 40 hours a week is night and day, believe me. While discipline and order are easy to maintain in the structured and sterile environment of your regular martial arts classes, it is nearly impossible to maintain that same atmosphere all day long.

If you run a camp, you will eventually have to deal with boredom, arguments, sick and injured kids, and other various mishaps that are too numerous to mention here. Dealing with these issues day-in and day-out can fray your nerves in short order. (However, there is one advantage to running a camp; it is an excellent form of birth control!

Shortly after we ran our first summer camp, my wife told me that she had decided she never wanted to have children.)

All kidding aside, *after-school and summer camps will end your cash flow worries* **if you do them right**. If you are interested in learning the right way to start a program in your school and want to avoid all the legal problems, there is a way to do it. I personally ran after-school and summer camps in my schools for over a decade, and I learned a lot about how to do it right during that time. If you want to know all the tips and tricks I learned during that time, visit After-SchoolKarateProgram.com for more information.

But I warn you; it is going to be a lot of work and you will need some starting capital in order to get your program off the ground. My advice is that you make sure you are up to the task before you commit to running a camp in your studio.

In Closing

That's essentially the bare bones basics of using MPCs to generate extra income for your studio. Only one more chapter to go! And, I saved the best for last (that's sarcasm, in case you didn't catch it...)

THIRTEEN

HIRING AND TRAINING HELP

Replacing Yourself without Bankrupting Your Martial Arts School

I was tempted to call this chapter "The Care and Feeding of Employees." However, I didn't want to give you the impression that all employees are bad. Hiring good help can be one of the best things that you can do to build your business; however, hiring the wrong help can bring you miseries that you have not imagined even in your worst nightmares.

It is important that you understand the "why's" and "how's" of hiring and training staff. I don't want you to make the same mistakes I have made and hire people for the wrong reasons. I also don't want you to make the mistake that many school owners make and hire people that you don't need. For some reason, the martial arts industry has gotten the notion that a martial arts studio has to have a lot of employees with fancy-sounding titles in order to be successful. This is simply not true, for a variety of reasons, some of which were already discussed in previous chapters.

There is one thing I want you to know before you decide to hire anyone to work in your business; that payroll can easily become your largest expense, if you don't keep close tabs on staffing and scheduling. **You really only need one additional employee in your studio, and that's someone to manage the office while you are on the floor.** And, you don't need to hire that person until you get up to about 100-125 active students; before reaching that point, you can get by with appointing an assistant from your student body to help you out in each class and take over briefly in case you have to answer the phone or greet a new prospect. Once you hit 100 students, however, you really need to consider hiring someone to handle those responsibilities for you.

One final thought here before I go on to the actual hiring process. You only have one goal when hiring a new employee and that is to find the most qualified and motivated individual for the position. You are not in business to do charity work; to help out your family, friends, or their family and friends; or to be nice to others and save the planet. You are in business to make a profit, plain and simple. Hiring an employee for any other reason than the fact that they are the most qualified person for a position is pure madness, and it will eventually cause you some grief. Do yourself a favor; hire for the right reasons.

Before You Hire Anyone...

There are many state and federal laws regulating the act of hiring and employing people in your business, and you need to be aware of them prior to beginning the process of hiring staff members. Running awry of these regulations has led to many a school owner finding themselves in hot water with local and state authorities. However, it's not hard to find out what you need to know before you hire; good places to start would be at the SBA website, at the IRS website, the Department of Labor website, at your state's labor or workforce commission website, and at the EEOC (Equal Employment Opportunity Commission) website. And of course, speak with your accountant.

Laws and regulations tend to change from state to state, but just to get you started here are a few things that you'll need to do to ensure that you are in compliance with local, state, and federal laws:

- First, get a federal employer identification number (EIN) by filing IRS Form SS-4 with the IRS.
- You will also have to learn how to file IRS Form 940-EZ, which is used to report your federal unemployment tax each year.
- You need to get into your accounting software program and set up the payroll system for calculating pay, withholding taxes and making payroll tax payments to the IRS.
- You should talk to your insurance agent about getting worker's compensation insurance.
- Become familiar with OSHA regulations.
- Make sure that you post all the federally required notices in a prominent place in your studio. Check with the Department of Labor and with your state employment office to find out which notices you have to post (In Texas we have the Texas Workforce Commission, but it may vary from state to state).
- In addition, check with the state labor agencies to find out what taxes and other withholding allowances need to be deducted from the employee's pay for unemployment, state tax, etc. Note that you have to match your employee's withholding, so speak with your accountant about how this will affect your profit margins.
- Also, meet with your accountant and attorney to discuss the various tax and legal issues surrounding the hire of new staff members.
- Finally, type up a suitable employment application. Be certain that it includes the following important questions:

✓ Are you 18 years of age or older?

✓ Are you legally authorized to work in the United States on a full-time basis?

✓ Do you currently use illegal drugs?

How to Recruit and Hire a New Employee

The first thing you need to figure out before you hire someone is simply what their job description and responsibilities will be. In other words, what exactly do you need them to do? The following is an example of a job description I pulled from the operations manual I used at my old studio; as you will see, this position entails a lot of work and a great deal of responsibility.

Job Description: Office Manager

The Office Manager is the reception and front office person. He or she is responsible for ensuring each client's satisfaction. This person must be very outgoing, polite, and friendly, because their primary responsibility is building rapport with clients and handling client satisfaction issues.

Characteristics of a great Office Manager are an ability to handle pressure well, be multi-task oriented, handle client concerns with grace and composure, and a very outgoing, polite, and friendly personality.

The Office Manager reports directly to the Chief Instructor or School Owner.

Job Responsibilities of the Office Manager are:

- *Meet and greet every new prospect that walks through the door in a polite and friendly manner.*
- *Answers the phones.*
- *Handles all calls and walk-ins concerning inquiries about lessons and services.*

- *Sets Intro Appointments.*
- *Makes confirmation calls on all intro appointments the day before the lesson.*
- *Sends notes out to confirm all appointments set.*
- *Creates a visible schedule of intro appointments, special events, and other activities for the Instructors (i.e., updating the calendar and keeping the Intro Appointment board current and up-to-date on a daily basis).*
- *Conducts Enrollment Conferences and Renewal Conferences (during class times and peak flow hours).*
- *Handles all merchandizing and display in Pro Shop area.*
- *Places all equipment orders every Thursday based on the equipment restocking inventory count.*
- *Alerts School Owner to all client issues concerning new students (45 days or less).*
- *Alerts Instructors to all client issues concerning established students (more than 45 days into their membership).*
- *Conducts the first round of MIA calls for Instructors on every Friday. Turns over any student with a problem that he or she is unable to resolve to the Chief Instructor or School Owner.*
- *Keeps Reception area and Pro Shop area neat and clean on a daily basis.*

Compensation: Hourly wage plus a bonus based on new enrollments and renewals personally completed.

The Next Step In Recruiting And Hiring: Pay

The next thing to do is to figure out what you are willing to pay to fill the position. My office manager was my girl Friday, handling all the administrative details while I was on the floor teaching. That's why I paid my office manager an hourly wage **plus** commission on her enrollments and renewals.

Basically, I set the hourly wage for the position to be comparable to what the local rate for administrative assistants was, and their commission was 10% of initial payments and $5.00 per renewal (we used an automatic renewal system on our memberships, which is why the commission was lower). In a good month, the Office Manager could pull down an extra $6-$10 per hour in commissions, and it was worth every penny for me to pay it. My recommendation to you is to set your hourly wages about 10-15% higher than the local rate, so you're not competing with other local businesses to retain your key employees.

After you figure out the job responsibilities and pay scale (make sure you can afford it) then you need to figure out how many hours this employee will work. For an Office Manager, 20-25 hours per week is sufficient. Like I said, you only need someone to work while you are on the floor, maybe from 3:00 PM to 8:00 PM Monday through Friday.

Recruiting and Job Posting

The next step is finding someone to fill the position. I highly recommend that you use both word-of-mouth and newspaper classifieds when you advertise the position. Also, be aware that when you advertise the job, you should not discriminate on the basis of race, gender, pregnancy, national origin, religion, disability and age. Although these are federal guidelines that generally apply to businesses with 15 or more employees, you would do well to avoid including anything in your ad that suggests discriminatory hiring practices of any kind.

Following advertising the position, you are going to have to start taking applications and setting up interviews. Make sure that every person who inquires about the job fills out an application for hire. Keep them on file in case you have to go back and prove that you followed a fair and equitable hiring procedure. Carefully review these applications and choose the top ten applicants for interviews. This may seem like a lot of interviews, but you want to make sure that you choose wisely from the largest applicant pool possible.

As for the interviews, you are going to want to make sure that you ask the right questions and say the right things:

- Avoid personalizing the job in your language. In other words, don't use language that gives the impression that the applicant already has the job.
- Explain the job and any specific requirements (hours, work load, pay range) at the beginning of the interview. Speak candidly and cut to the chase; it is best to weed out unqualified or "prima donna" applicants in the beginning of an interview so you don't waste time on those who are unqualified or that have conflicts with these issues.
- Ask open-ended questions that would give you a good indication of how sharp the applicant is. For instance, "How well do you handle heavy workloads?"
- Avoid asking questions that refer to discriminatory hiring practices.

After you complete your interviews, you should evaluate all applicants based on their qualifications and interview. If you have to narrow it down between two candidates, you can ask for references or just call the people they listed on their application. Once you have a likely candidate, call them back for a follow up interview to be sure you want to hire them. If it goes well, offer them a position at the end of the follow up interview, and keep them on a probationary hire status for at least 90 days, in case they don't work out. If they turn out to be lacking in certain areas, don't hesitate to can them and start calling back the other applicants that you turned down.

Other Considerations

After you have hired your new employee, there are a few more things you will need to do during their orientation:

- Make sure that they fill out an I-9 (from the USCIS) and an IRS W-4 Form, and make certain you get photocopies of the required forms of identification from the new hire.
- Have them sign a non-disclosure and non-compete agreement. Be aware that non-competes are not allowed in some states, so check with your attorney before you ask them to sign it.
- Sit down and give them an orientation on your policies and procedures manual. Then, give them a copy and have them sign a notice that states the date and time they received their orientation on your company's policies and procedures.
- Have them sign a copy of their job description and responsibilities.
- Plan to spend a full week training them for their job. Set aside specific times every day for training. Ease them into their position by assigning them basic tasks, and gradually adding responsibilities over their first four weeks. Do not overload them with too many things to remember all at once! Easing them into the position will ensure that they learn their job correctly and that they don't become frustrated and quit.

The Alternative to Hiring: Developing a Team of Volunteer Helpers

There is a lot of lip service given to developing "SWAT" or Leadership Teams to act as volunteers in a martial arts studio. I can tell you for a fact that it is harder than it sounds. It can be difficult to find students who are devoted enough to spend their spare time volunteering to help out in your studio during functions and events.

My advice to you is to make sure that you create an atmosphere that promotes and rewards volunteer help from day one. Make it known that at a certain rank it is a requirement for students to assist the instructor and that students that show outstanding talent and effort will be selected for additional duties.

In addition, make it clear that students who outrank other students are expected to help the lower ranking students in learning their techniques. This is just like the old "sempai-kohai" relationships that a lot of Japanese stylists are already familiar with. Foster an atmosphere where the advanced students know that they are expected to help out, and you will find it very easy to get free help.

You should also make it an honor and a privilege to serve in the position of sempai or senior student. Select one person in each class to be your right hand, and make a big deal out of it when you select them. Let them know that you picked them because they display the qualities that you desire in an assistant, and recognize them on a regular basis for their efforts. Remember the lesson we learned in the first few chapters of this book; people will work much harder for recognition than they will for monetary benefits.

Also, hold special classes every month for your helpers. In these classes, always cover something that they normally wouldn't get to learn or practice. You might also let them wear a special patch or uniform that designates them as part of the leadership team. Finally, spend time with them and teach them how to lead and how to teach; someday, you might even be hiring them to teach for you full-time.

For more information on the topic of training and hiring staff, I suggest you read another of my books titled *Developing Staff and Leadership Teams: How to Run and Grow Your Martial Arts School Efficiently With Minimal Staff and Payroll Overhead*, available on Amazon.com.

Managing and Leading Your Staff

There is not really one best management approach, but there are some that work better than others. Here are a few tips to guide you in your role as leader and mentor over your staff:

- **Treat your staff with respect.** Don't correct them in front of others, and praise them when do they things right. In short, use the same techniques that we discussed in the "Teaching Great Classes" section when you are training and correcting your staff.

- **Recognize and reward them.** Have a "helper of the month" program, give your helpers cards and gifts on their birthday and around the holidays, and let them attend seminars and purchase equipment at a discounted rate.

- **Lead from the front.** Anything you ask of your staff and helpers, you should be willing to do yourself.

- **Schedule quarterly and yearly reviews, and follow through on conducting them.** Your staff members need regular, structured feedback in order to grow and mature in their role.

- **Find out their goals.** In addition, you need to know what their goals are so you can assess how they fit into your organization. Don't expect your staff to just blurt out their aspirations; ask them specifically what they are. If it fits within your business goals, work with them in achieving their personal goals.

- **Listen to input.** Listen to your employee's concerns and accept their input. Asking their opinion will boost their confidence, and you might be surprised at how useful some of their ideas are. Be sure to address their concerns by trying to find solutions that fit with your business plan.

- **Stand firm and remember – you're in charge.**
  However, don't feel as though you have to implement any
  idea that your employees present to you. Strong leaders
  let it be known that their word is the final say in any
  decision-making situation.
- **Set boundaries.** Beware of employees that try to
  usurp your authority, or that take too much initiative. Set
  boundaries as to when an employee can act
  independently, and when they need to consult you
  before taking action.
- **Clear expectations.** On a related note, make sure
  that every employee and helper knows exactly what is
  expected of them, and have a written policy for
  infractions such as excessive absences and tardiness.
- **Treat everyone the same.** Be fair, but be firm and
  consistent when disciplining your employees. Avoid
  choosing favorites.
- **Volunteers are just that, so treat them
  accodingly.** Remember to go easy on your helpers; they
  are just volunteers!

Final Thoughts on Hiring and Training Staff

That concludes the section on hiring and training staff. I am a firm
believer in keeping your payroll down by using as much free help as
possible and by keeping your staff to a bare minimum. While it may
seem like a good idea to hire as many employees as you can afford,
remember that each employee costs a whole lot more than just their
hourly wage. You have to match part of their taxes and withholdings,
it costs you time and money to train them, it takes time and money to
manage them, and they can quit at the worst possible times. Take my
advice and keep your paid staff down to no more than two people,
and I can guarantee that you'll never be sorry you did so.

EPILOGUE

At some time in your career as a professional martial arts instructor and school owner you are going to suddenly realize, "Wow, I actually made it!" It will probably be about the time that you purchase your dream home, buy a new car, or take your family on a vacation you've always wanted to take. And let me tell you, there's no better feeling than when you're getting paid well to do what you love.

However, it takes hard work and sacrifice to get there. The first year or two after I opened my doors, I lived hand to mouth on a regular basis. Of course, I was doing a lot of things wrong at that time – I had not yet developed this business system. Still, you have to accept the fact that you are going to experience some rough times when you first start out. Long days and sleepless nights are going to become second nature to you.

Eventually, however, the difficulties will start to come less and less frequently, and the rewards will increase and come more often. At that time, you'll look back and say to yourself, "I'm glad that I took that first step; I'm glad that I followed my dream; I'm glad that I persevered and saw this through; *I am glad that I had the guts to do it.*"

I would like to hear about your triumphs because I care deeply about your success. Please, send me an email, drop me a postcard, or write me a letter to tell me about your success stories. I can be reached at:

Mike Massie

P.O. Box 682

Dripping Springs, TX 78620

Or, you may contact me via my blog at:

MartialArtsBusinessDaily.com

APPENDICES

Remember, **if you don't measure it, you can't improve it.**
So, at the very minimum you need to track your leads, appointments,
no-shows, enrollments, and drop-outs every month, and compare
them with the following benchmarks in order to ensure you are
staying on track in growing your school.

Lead generation:

- Minimum 30 leads per month
- 15-20 from website
- 10-15 from other leads sources (guest passes, door
  hangers, etc.)

Appointments:

- 80% of leads should set an appointment for an intro
  lesson or free class
- Or, 24 of those 30 leads should set an appointment

No-Shows:

- About 20% of your appointments will be no-shows
- Or, about 19 of those 24 people should show up for a free class or intro lesson

Enrollments:

- 80% of those students who take an intro lesson or attend a guest class should enroll
- Or, about 15 of those 19 people who take an intro lesson or free class should enroll on a membership

Attrition:

- Your attrition rate should average 3% per month over the course of a year
- Or, with an enrollment of 100 students, no more than 3 of those students should drop out each month

Enrollment Projections and Attrition

We want to enroll at least 15 new students a month, converting leads to enrollments at a minimum 50% conversion rate, with about 60% of our leads coming from our website and the rest coming from other lead sources. Accounting for a 3% attrition rate, hitting these bare minimum lead generation, enrollment, and retention numbers will still ensure that we are able to grow our studio at a steady pace. Theoretically, *if you started with just 40 students* **your school would grow to over 175 students at the end of 12 months**, just by hitting these benchmarks.

However, keeping your retention rates high and your attrition low is critical to your growth. If your attrition rate were at 5% per month, at the end of that same 12 month period you would only have

153 students. And if it were 10%, with the same enrollment numbers you'd just have 108 students at the end of 12 months. So, once you have your marketing system in place and you are hitting your appointment setting and sales percentages it's time to focus on retention, because it will quickly become the key to your sustained growth.

Incidentally, the gross tuition collections for a school hitting those benchmarks are as follows:

Starting Enrollment:

- Month 0: 40 Students @ $149/mo. Tuition = $5,960.00

3% Attrition:

- Month 12: 176 Students @ $149/mo. Tuition = $26,224.00

5% Attrition:

- Month 12: 153 Students @ $149/mo. Tuition = $22,797.00

10% Attrition:

- Month 12: 108 Students @ $149/mo. Tuition = $16,092.00

Trouble-Shooting Problem Areas

How to Address Common Problem Areas:

- **Not Enough Leads** - If you aren't getting enough

leads, you need to *improve or increase* your marketing. Review Chapter 10.

- **Not Enough Appointments** - If you aren't setting enough appointments, you need to improve your phone skills. Review Chapter 8.
- **No-Shows** - If you're getting a lot of no-shows, you need to start verifying your appointments the day before. And, you may need to improve your phone skills as well.
- **Enrollments** - If you aren't converting a high percentage of intro lessons to enrollments, you need to improve your sales skills (or your classes are boring). Review Chapter 8.
- **Drop-Outs** - If your attrition rates are high, this could be due to multiple factors. First, are you using contracts? If you are, then the most likely causes of your retention issues are boring classes, students who don't perceive that they are making progress toward their goals, or students who feel as though you don't care about them. Working on the teaching skills and retention strategies from Chapter 11 will go a long way toward improving your retention and lowering your attrition rates.
- **Late-Paying Clients** - Switch to electronic payments exclusively, and only take cash or checks for initial payments.
- **High Enrollment/Attendance But Low Cash-Flow** - You either need to raise your rates, or you're taking too many cash-outs and squandering that income. Need I say more?
- **Instructor Burnout** - You're obviously working too much. First, unless you have someone to teach them for you, don't schedule weekend classes; you need time off each week to rest. Second, take a vacation. And I mean a vacation from everything. To accomplish this end, I close my schools two weeks out of the year for vacation; one

week at Christmas and one week in July. That way, I don't even have to *think* about work while I'm on vacation. I also close my school on all bank and federal holidays. Finally, train some staff to help you. Review Chapter 13 and read my book titled *Developing Staff and Leadership Teams*, available at Amazon.com.

Additional Resources

More Books By Mike Massie

For more books by Mike Massie on achieiving martial arts business success, visit his author page at:

Amazon.com/author/mikemassie

Recommended Reading

The following books are recommended for personal and business development.

On Developing a Prosperity Mindset

- *The Millionaire Next Door* by Thomas J. Stanley and William D. Danko
- *Think and Grow Rich* by Napoleon Hill
- *Retire Young, Retire Rich* by Robert Kiyosaki and Sharon Lechter
- Other books in the *Rich Dad, Poor Dad* series
- *Multiple Streams of Income* by Robert G. Allen

On Marketing and Selling

- *Secrets of Closing the Sale* by Zig Ziglar
- *How to Get Publicity* by William Parkhurst
- *Write Great Ads, A Step-by-Step Approach* by Erica Levy Klein
- *Getting Everything You Can Out of All You've Got* by Jay Abraham

On Management and Dealing with People

- *Personality Plus* by Florence Littauer
- *Peopleware* by Tom DeMarco and Tim Lister

Martial Arts General Reference

- *Living the Martial Way* by Forrest Morgan
- *Martial Arts America* by Bob Orlando
- *The Martial Arts Athlete* by Tom Seabourne
- *The Bare Essentials Guide for Martial Arts Injury Care and Prevention* by Trish Bare Grounds
- *The Science of Martial Arts Training* by Charles Staley

For Sample Forms and Documents

For access to my entire archive of martial arts school management sample forms and documents, including:

- Waiver forms

- Membership agreements
- Class schedules
- Ads and marketing documents
- Event fliers
- Staff and hiring documents
- Program description handouts
- And much more...

...then visit MartialArtsBusinessU.com to get started today. By doing so you'll have access to tons of ads, documents, forms, and content to help you grow your dojo, and at a very reasonable cost.

ABOUT THE AUTHOR

Mike Massie is the author of
Small Dojo Big Profits and has
been a professional martial arts
instructor for over twenty years.
Mr. Massie holds dan ranks in Sil
Jeon Mu Sul, Moo Duk Kwan,
Tae Kwon Do, Hapkido,
Shotokan, and Jujutsu, and has
been studying and training in the
martial arts since 1984.

Mr. Massie graduated from St.
Edward's University in 2004 with a Bachelor's degree in Allied
Health Science and a Minor in Business Administration. He is the
creator of Fighting Fit Boot Camp and The Self Defense Black Belt
Program. He is also a certified personal fitness trainer with the
National Exercise and Sports Trainers Association (lifetime) and a
certified kettlebell coach.

Through his materials, including his manuals, articles, websites,
blog, and newsletter, Mr. Massie has helped thousands of martial arts
instructors achieve greater financial success, while finding increased
personal satisfaction in their careers as professional martial artists.

Mr. Massie lives with his family in Austin, Texas.